PLATO'S APOLOGY OF SOCRATES

A New Translation, in the Style of a Cinematic Novella

Translated & Cinematized by
Steve Kostecke

All translations & cinematic additions
by Steve Kostecke

ISBN-10: 1456490613
ISBN-13: 978-1456490614

Contents

Extracts from
The Oath of an Athenian Juror

I will vote for a verdict
in accordance with the laws
and the democratic decrees
of the Athenian Assembly
and the Council of Five Hundred.

I will hear out both
the prosecution and the defense
in an equal manner, impartially,
and cast my vote
without favor or enmity.

I swear this oath by
Zeus, Poseidon, and Demeter,
and a curse of ruin
will be on myself
and on my household
if I should break this oath in any way.

The blessings of fortune depend on
keeping true to my word.

Plato's Apology of Socrates

a Cinematic Novella

Time

Midmorning, a day in 399BC.

Place

Interior of a courthouse in Athens.

People

Socrates: the accused.
Several companions of Socrates.
Meletus, Anytus, Lycon: the accusers.
A jury of 500 men over thirty years of age.
A standing-room only crowd of male spectators.
Magistrate, clerk, herald: courtroom officials.
Two members of the Eleven prison authority.
Two armed guards.

[Cinematic additions are in brackets.]

Plato's *Apology of Socrates* is unbracketed.

The Courtroom

[Open with a view of the *bēma* – the speaker's platform, three meters by two – and of the young man standing at its center with his arm rigidly aimed in the direction of the man he has just accused. He stands fixed in position for several moments – the eyes and nose of a hawk peering out between two black sheets of shoulder-length hair – until he is certain that his words have sunk into the ears of everyone present. He then relaxes his arm and lets it dangle at the side of his calf-length *chiton*, clean and white and fastened about his waist with a cord of beige cloth. Seated behind him on the platform, on a wooden bench set against the wall, are two other men. One of them is also a young man in a white sleeveless tunic tied neatly at the waist; the other is a man in his fifties with gilt embroidery running along the edges of his indigo *chiton*. The wall they are seated against is itself one of the long sides of the rectangular courtroom – twenty meters by forty – with the *bēma* jutting out at its middle, three steps high.

[Cut to a view of the courtroom as seen from the *bēma*. In the space in front of the platform – between it and the jury seating area – sit the three court officials. The court magistrate is seated on a wooden chair with a large curvature at the top of its back, the ends of the curved board sticking out on each side of the magistrate's shoulders. On one side of the magistrate is the court herald, sitting with a contraption at his feet consisting of two vertical poles supporting a horizontal pole. The horizontal pole holds twelve wooden rings. At the moment, several of the rings are at one end of the pole and the rest are at the other end. On the opposite side of the magistrate is the court clerk, sitting with a writing table in front of him. On the table are sheets of papyrus, a reed quill, an inkwell and a blotting cloth; underneath the table, at his feet, is a very low wide-rimmed ceramic container with a lid on top of it. Behind the courtroom officials, in three trapezoidal sections slanting upward toward the back of the room, sit the five hundred jury members on wooden benches. Most of them have removed their cloaks and draped them over their bench spaces, revealing a motley patchwork of differently-colored *chitons*. Although the five hundred men come from all levels of Athenian society, the lower economic rungs are represented most among them – those with sporadic or seasonal work, for instance – due to jury duty being an all-volunteer affair with the pay of half-a-day's minimum wage as the reward. Because of this, the earthier-colored *chitons* – the browns and grays and rust-reds preferred by those who work with animals and farm the land – predominate in the crowd. Low narrow stairways run up between each trapezoidal section and against each wall to the spectator area at the upper back of the courtroom. Behind the wooden railing that separates the jury members from this area is a standing-room only crowd of men, with many of them spilling out from the area and standing on the uppermost steps along each wall. Above their heads and further to the back is a series of windows that run along the four walls at an even height. Sounds can faintly be heard from the neighboring agora, the central marketplace and meeting place of any Greek city-state.

[Cut back to the view of the *bēma*. The two men seated on the bench behind the young man stand up, and the elder man dressed in gilt-embroidered indigo leads as the three of them somberly step down the platform toward the bench for the prosecution. The court herald steps up onto the *bēma* and asks if there is anyone who challenges the testimony that was presented by the accusers. No one replies. The herald then announces that the prosecution has rested its case and that the defendant will now be given twelve *choes* of time to make his defense. He gestures toward the *clepsydra*, the water-clock. Cut to the *clepsydra* located in a corner near one of the guarded doorways, with a dozen large and small amphoras filled with water lined against the wall next to it. The juryman who has been allotted the task of operating the water-clock plugs the thin copper spout coming out from the bottom of the upper jar – a six-liter jar equal to two *choes*, which takes roughly twelve minutes to empty, – lifts the bottom jar up and pours its contents back into the upper one. He replaces the lower jar and looks at the herald. Cut back to the view from the speaker's platform as the herald descends the platform, returns to his seat next to the court magistrate and slides the wooden rings of his device so that they are all together at one end of the horizontal pole.

[Cut to a mid-court view of the *bēma*, with the bench for the prosecution to the right of it and the bench for the defense to the left. Sitting on the defense bench are half a dozen men: two of them about thirty years old, one of them middle-aged, and three of them well into their later years. One of the elderly men rises up and walks toward the platform. He's somewhat stout and squat with a slight paunch noticeable beneath the folds of his sooty ankle-length *chiton*. He has a curling white beard, a balding head, thick lips, bulging eyes, a pug nose – an almost comically ugly face. His light-gray cloak – not much darker than his well-worn tunic – is wrapped across his chest and draped over one shoulder. Cut to a close-up of his bare, weathered feet taking the three steps up the *bēma*, with the sound of his rough soles scraping against the stone. Cut back to a mid-court view of Socrates standing calmly poised in the center of the platform, his large eyes shining. The herald – as seen from behind – motions toward the man at the *clepsydra* in the corner. Cut to a close-up of the plug being removed from the copper spout as the flow of water and time begins. Cut back to Socrates on the *bēma*, without anyone or anything else in view.]

Opening Remarks

Socrates

What you have just experienced at the hands of my accusers – and what effect it had on you, Athenians, – I can only imagine. They spoke so persuasively that I nearly forgot who I was *myself* because of them, … [Socrates sweeps his arm toward the prosecution bench.] … and yet hardly a word of truth came out of their mouths.

> [Cut to the bench for the prosecution. The faces of the two youthful accusers scowl; the older man maintains a prideful gaze. Cut back to the view of the *bēma*.]

Of all their many lies about me, there is one in particular that astonished me most: when they told you that you had better be on your guard – keep your wits about you – and not allow yourselves to be deceived by me, such a crafty and clever speaker am I. The fact that they showed not the slightest shame in stating this – especially since they are about to be proven wrong by what I do and say here today, when I do not come across that way whatsoever, – *this* to me was the most appalling thing from them. ... [Socrates tilts his head slightly.] ... Unless, of course, they happen to be calling crafty and clever anyone who *speaks the truth*. If this is what they mean, then I would have to agree that I am an orator of sorts, but definitely not of *their* sort. As I said, these men, ... [Socrates points his hand at the three of them, the fingers of his hand clasped together.] ... they have hardly uttered a word of truth. ... [He lowers his arm and stares intently at the crowd.] ... But from me you *will* hear the truth and *nothing but* the truth. And certainly not, by Zeus, in language that has been so finely-adorned like theirs, with their words and phrases so carefully selected and arranged. You will hear my speech being spoken *at random*, unprepared, using whatever words that happen to come to me – with full trust they will come out correct and just, – and not one of you should expect otherwise. It would hardly be appropriate of me to stand here before you at my age and make up stories ... [Socrates directs his arm again at the prosecution.] ... *like a juvenile boy.*

[Cut to the prosecution bench. The young man with the hawk-like nose and eyes intensifies his scowl and glare. Return to Socrates on the speaker's platform.]

One thing I must ask of you – *beg of you*, in fact, men of Athens, – is that if you hear me speaking in my defense in the same manner as you have heard me speak in the agora near the exchange tables ... [Visual of Socrates in the vicinity of the money-changers – surrounded by the bustle of the market-place, conversing animatedly with several men, dressed exactly as he is in court this day, – while the following is heard spoken:] – where so many of you have heard me speak, as well as elsewhere [Return to the *bēma*.] ... – do not be shocked or shout out on account of that. The situation I find myself in this morning is that for the first time in my life I have come before a court of law – at seventy years of age – and I am entirely foreign to the types of speech that are given here. And just as I would expect from you if I *were* in fact a foreigner from another land – that you would surely be understanding and forgiving of me if I spoke in the language and mannerisms in which I had been raised, – *that* is what I ask of you now, as seems only fair to me. Allow me to speak in my customary manner – for however better or worse it may be, – and consider my words carefully while keeping your minds focused on this single point: *whether what I say is just or not.* ... [Socrates lifts his palm till it comes level with the seating area of the jurors.] ... This is, after all, the virtue of a juryman, ... [The fingers fold back above his palm to become directed at himself.] ... just as speaking the truth is that of anyone who speaks to our citizens in public.

> [Socrates lowers his arm and glances solemnly around the courtroom for several moments. Although the room is constantly filled with murmurs, sounds from the agora and the movement of bodies on the creaking benches, it is quiet enough at the moment for the trickle from the *clepsydra* to be heard echoing from its corner. Cut to the corner with the water-clock. The juryman in charge of it is sitting on a tripod stool – on top of his cloak which is doubled-up and draped over it, – leaning forward with both elbows on his knees. Cut back to Socrates on the *bēma*.]

Statement of the Case

Socrates

It would only be right of me, Athenians, to begin by defending myself against my earlier accusers and the first and original false allegations that were made against me, then turn to the more recent allegations … [Socrates motions toward the prosecution.] … and these men here who have made them. I have had my fair share of accusers in the past – many of them, in fact, over many years – who have told you nothing true about me, but they cause me much greater fear and concern than Anytus and his backers, … [He turns his gaze toward their bench. Cut to Anytus, the older man dressed in the fine indigo fabric, seated between the two young men, while the following is heard spoken:] fearsome as they are.

> [Cut from the real-time of the courtroom. Flashback to the battle of Pylos during the Peloponnesian War, twenty-five years earlier. Anytus, in the armor and gear of a general, is standing behind an earthwork rampart above a shoreline, directing a group of archers. At his command they release a volley of arrows. Cut to the view from the rampart. Dozens of Spartan soldiers are disembarking from their landing boats – several Spartan triremes seen anchored off-shore in the middle of a bay – and are charging up the sands. The arrows arc through the air, hitting several of their targets. Return to the real-time of the courtroom and Anytus seated on the prosecution bench, a look of pride indelibly etched onto his face. Cut back to Socrates on the *bēma*.]

Those who concern me much more, Athenians, are those who had charge of you from childhood on up, who raised and counseled so many of you, indoctrinating you against me. They vilified me in front of you with no more truth to their accusations than those of these men here today, telling you such things as: "There is a man named Socrates, a so-called wise man, ... [Visuals of: the stage at an outdoor amphitheater, with an actor in a grinning mask rocking back and forth in a wicker basket held up by the ropes of a stage-crane, waving an arm back and forth ecstatically while proclaiming to be treading the air and investigating the sun; then the view from behind the actor, with the expanse of the semi-circular seating area visible, as the audience is seen to burst into laughter, while the following is heard spoken:] a thinker of the mysteries in the skies and beneath the earth, who has sought out and pried into all things imaginable, and knows the trick of making the weaker argument stronger." [Return to Socrates on the *bēma*.] ... The men who cast these aspersions on me, Athenians, they are the ones who are *truly* frightening to me, since whoever listens to them surely believes that anyone who searches into such matters must be beyond believing in the gods. And not only are they numerous – these men who have been reviling me for so many years now, – but they also told you these things at an age when you would be most susceptible to believing them, when you were either children or slightly older. And to make matters worse, all of this was done without anyone there to give a defense, making me guilty by default. ... [A look of reproach forms on his face.] ... But what I think is the most ridiculous and unfair part of all is that I have no way of knowing who these accusers are or of speaking any of their names – unless, of course, one of them happens to be a comic playwright.

[Cut from the real-time of the courtroom back to the amphitheater. The playwright Aristophanes, who's standing in the seating area after the play, holds up the mask of Socrates next to the face of the man himself. The three of them – Aristophanes, the mask of Socra-

18

tes, and the middle-aged Socrates – each have a grin. The theater-goers around them burst into laughter. Return to real-time and Socrates on the *bēma*.]

All of the men who constantly strove to mislead you with their personal resentment and insults – or those who had their own heartstrings plucked without knowing me and then went about plucking others', – all of these men are most difficult, if not *impossible*, for me to deal with. I cannot bring any of them here before you and question him. Instead, I am completely forced into defending myself as if fighting against shadows, cross-examining the air with no one to reply.

[Socrates glances derisively around the courtroom for several moments. He then relaxes his features and resumes speaking in a gentler manner.]

So grant me what I say, that I have two sets of accusers – those who have just now made charges against me and those that did so long ago, – and surely you see the need for me to address the charges of my earlier accusers first, since you heard their accusations first and with much greater impact than the later charges from these men here.

[Socrates stares out at his listeners, observing the reactions on their faces. Cut to an area of jurors as they placidly stare back at him. Cut back to Socrates, who continues in a resolute tone.]

Very well, then, Athenians, I must defend myself against the earlier charges and attempt to remove the bias and prejudice that has taken hold of your minds over such a long period of time – and do this in such a *short* period of time.

[Cut to a close-up of the *clepsydra* and the trickle of water and time running out from its copper spout into the lower jar. Return to Socrates on the *bēma*.]

While I certainly have hopes of this happening and I succeed in clearing my name – if anything could be better for both you and me, – I am fully aware, all the same, of what a difficult task this is. ... [Socrates shakes his head.] ... The nature of what lies before me does not escape me at all.

[Socrates' eyes lift up and catch sight of something at the far back of the courtroom. Cut to the row of windows at the upper back of the room, above the spectators' heads. The outline of a bird can be seen – black against the luminous sky – perched on one of the sills. It rests motionless for a moment; then in a sudden flurry it flies away. Cut back to Socrates on the platform as he brings his glance back down to the level of his judges.]

Whatever the outcome may be, though, let it go whichever way pleases the gods. The law must be obeyed and I must make my case.

[Cut from the real-time of the courtroom. Flashback to a scene near the exchange tables in the agora a few days before the trial. Socrates is in the middle of a philosophic discussion with several men. They're debating whether or not it is the duty of a citizen to obey the laws of his city in the same way as it is a child's duty to obey the commands of his parents. Socrates is arguing in support of this notion. One of the men present – named Hermogenes – suddenly interrupts the discussion to ask why Socrates is exerting so much effort on this topic rather than preparing his defense for his upcoming trial. With a gleam in his eyes, Socrates informs him that his entire life has been a preparation for his defense. Hermogenes asks him what he means. Socrates replies that he has led a virtuous life and has always avoided any wrong-doing – which is the best defense that any man can have. Cut back to the real-time of the courtroom and the view of the *bēma*.]

Defense Against the Earlier Charges

Socrates

Taking it up from the start, what exactly are the allegations that give rise to my bad name, ... [Socrates points his palm, fingers clasped together, toward the young man with the characteristics of a bird of prey.] ... the ones that Meletus trusts in so deeply as to bring his indictment against me?

[Cut to Meletus, seated to one side of Anytus, staring fiercely from the prosecution bench. Cut back to Socrates on the platform.]

What is it, then, that the vilifiers say when they vilify me? Just as plaintiffs are required to make a sworn statement, theirs would go something like this: "Socrates is guilty of wrong-doing. He puts too much time and effort into searching into the mysteries beneath the earth and in the heavens and making the weaker argument stronger, and he is wrong for teaching these very things to other people." You have witnessed these accusations yourselves in the comedy of Aristophanes – some man named Socrates swinging about in a basket proclaiming to be traipsing along the air, ... [Visual of a close-up of the actor in the Socrates mask flailing an arm while rocking back and forth in the wicker basket, while the following is heard spoken:] and uttering a whole lot of other nonsense about things that I do not pretend to have the slightest knowledge about. [Cut back to the courtroom.] ... Far be it for me, though, to disparage this type of knowledge, if there is anyone who is wise when it comes to such matters ... [Socrates gives a sidelong glance at the bench for the prosecution.] ... – and may Meletus not drag me before a court of law for so great an offense as claiming to be such a person – but as for inquiries of this sort, Athenians, I have nothing to do with them. In fact, as witnesses to this, I call on many of you yourselves. I think it worthwhile at this moment for all of you who have ever heard me in my discussions – since there are so many of you who have – to speak out right now and let your fellow jurymen know if any of you have ever heard me discussing such things at length or even once in passing.

[Socrates stops and glares out at the five hundred jury members. Cut to a view of the jury area as seen from the bēma. Many of the jurors twist their heads back and forth to see if anyone has stood up to speak. No one has. Cut back to Socrates as he confidently nods his head.]

And from this response you can just as well reach the conclusion that the other allegations most people make against me are of the same sort – *none of them is true.* And if any of you have heard that I put my time and effort into trying to teach people and make money from that, this is false as well ... [He gives a slight tilt to his head.] ... – though such an effort seems perfectly good to me if somebody has the ability to teach as the sophists do. Gorgias of Leontini, Prodicus of Ceos, Hippias of Ellis: each of these men, Athenians, has the ability to persuade young men to gather around him in each and every city he enters, ... [Visual of a sophist lecturing in the colonnaded walkway of a building adjacent to an agora, young men surrounding him and listening intently, as the following is heard spoken:] young men who can spend their time with any *fellow* citizen they wish for free. These young men leave behind their usual companions to flock around him, [Visual of one of the young men placing a few coins into the palm of the sophist and then placing his hand on his chest and bowing slightly, as the following is heard spoken:] giving him their money and their thanks as well.

[Return to Socrates on the platform as his face brightens with recollection.]

Now that I think of it, there is another man known for his wisdom I recently found out is in Athens these days, a man from the isle of Paros. I learned he was in our city when I happened to run into a man who has spent more money on sophists than all other men combined, Callias the son of Hipponicos. I asked him the following, since he has two sons: "Callias," I said, "if your sons happened to be colts or calves and we had to seek out and hire a trainer for them – a person who would raise them to be excellent in the virtues of their kind, – this man would most likely be a horse-trainer or a farmer. But since your boys are human, who do you have in mind to take as their trainer and teacher? Who is it that is both knowledgeable and skilled in virtues such as the goodness of a man and a citizen? My guess is that you have already thought about this on account of your sons, so is there anyone who is able to impart such knowledge and virtues to them," I asked, "or perhaps not?" "There most certainly is," he told me. "Who, and from where?" I asked; "And what does he charge for his teaching?" "Evenus of Paros, Socrates," he told me, "for five minas."

[Muffled laughs spurt out throughout the crowd – a mina of silver being roughly equal to a year's pay at minimum wage. Socrates maintains an earnest expres-

23

sion, recalling how the renowned sophist, Protagoras, used to charge as much as 100 minas for his tutorship in the prosperous days before the War.]

And I thought to myself what a fortunate and happy man Evenus must be if he truly had such talent and was able to teach virtues and excellence at such a modest cost. I myself would puff up with pride and pretentions if I understood what Evenus apparently does ... [His earnestness intensifies.] ... – but, Athenians, I tell you that *I do not have such knowledge.*

[The trickle from the *clepsydra*, which has been faintly droning in the background, stops. Cut to the water-clock. The juryman in charge of it stands up, plugs the copper spout and lifts up the bottom jar. He pours the six liters of water back into the upper jar and sets the bottom jar back in its place. He then removes the plug, and the stream of water and time continues. Cut to the herald in his seat next to the court magistrate. He slides two of the wooden rings on his contraption to one side of the horizontal pole. Cut back to Socrates on the *bēma* as he lifts his eyes from the herald's device to the jury in front of him.]

Now perhaps one of you might take me up on this point and say: "Socrates, what is it that you have done, then? Where has all of this bias and prejudice against you come from? It certainly cannot be the case that you have done nothing out of the ordinary and still such widespread rumors and rumblings have risen up – unless you were, in fact, engaged in activities that were quite different from everyone else. So tell us what it is, or else we might jump to a wrong conclusion." This seems perfectly fair for anyone to say, so I will try to show you what it is that has given rise to all of the slander and lies about me. Do listen carefully, and even though it will seem like I am joking around and not being serious to some of you, know fully well that what I will tell you *is* the complete truth.

[Socrates stops for a moment and stands motionless on the *bēma*. His eyes are directed forward but don't appear to be fixed on anything. This blank stare continues until he blinks and his focus returns to the men seated in front of him. He slowly nods his head.]

I have, in fact, Athenians, gained my notoriety due to nothing other than *an actual type of wisdom*.

[Socrates scans the courtroom for reactions. The undertones and murmuring go silent. The trickle from the *clepsydra* becomes amplified for several moments.]

What kind of wisdom am I talking about? A type of *human* wisdom, to be sure. In reality it must be this type and nothing more. Those men I was just talking about – the sophists, – perhaps *they* might be wise with some type of wisdom greater than the human kind, ... [His head tilts briefly.] ... or I have no way of explaining it, but *I* certainly do not have that type of wisdom myself, and anyone who says that I do is both lying and trying to fill you with contempt for me.

[Socrates pauses and glances cautiously around the silent courtroom.]

And let me remind you again, Athenians, not to shout out and interrupt me, not even if I sound like I am bragging or talking big about myself, because what I am about to tell you – the account of myself I will relate – is not my own but comes from a source that you surely hold as worthy of your trust and credibility. Regarding my claim to ... [He stops himself from finishing the phrase.] ... – *if*, in fact, anyone is wise, and in whatever way, – I am presenting to you as a witness the god in Delphi, *Apollo himself.*

[Gasps and skeptical groans are released. They immediately rise up into a general commotion. One man
yells out that this is sacrilege; another man shouts that
such a witness is not possible; and another man demands to know what kind of comedy is being acted
out here? Nodding his head, Socrates lifts up his arm,
palm raised, until the uproar begins to subside. He
continues once his voice can be clearly heard again.]

I suppose that most of you here are familiar with Chaerephon.
He was a close friend of mine from youth – and a friend of the
democracy, taking part in the exile with so many of you during the reign of the Thirty.

[Cut from the real-time of the courtroom. Flashback to
five years earlier, at the end of the Peloponnesian War,
with a scene of the Spartan army breaching the walls of
Athens in their final drive for victory. Cut next to a
scene of the Spartan soldiers racing up the wide stair-
case of the Acropolis toward the Parthenon – the temple to Athena, the patron goddess of Athens, – in order
to ransack the city treasury. Cut next to a scene of the
Spartan generals assembling the Thirty Tyrants in the
Rotunda – the city hall of Athens, – thirty pro-Spartan,
anti-democracy Athenians who will rule Athens at
Sparta's command. Cut next to a scene in the Rotunda
with several of the tyrants presiding over a vote: Athenian citizens file in to partake in the vote, dropping a
voting-pebble into one of two large urns on the floor of
the circular chamber – one wooden, the other one
made of bronze, – while the tyrants scrutinize each
person and the vote they make. Cut next to a scene of
armed Athenians storming the Rotunda in order to
commence the overthrow of the tyrants. As the battal-
ion rushes in, cut to a group of men standing outside of
the Rotunda, men who are evidently leaders in the in-

26

surrection. Cut to a close-up of Anytus standing staunchly among these men. Cut back to the real-time of the courtroom and Anytus seated on the prosecution bench, gazing at Socrates with an air of pride and self-importance. Cut back to Socrates on the *bēma*.]

Chaerephon returned with you, as well, once the democracy was restored. And certainly many of you remember what kind of man he was, how energetically he plunged into whatever inspired him. On one occasion in particular he took it on himself to go to Delphi in order to ask the oracle – and as I have said, men of Athens, keep yourselves from shouting out and interrupting me, – he asked the oracle of Delphi if anyone were *wiser than I am*. And the Pythian Priestess offered up this response: ... [Visual of the interior of the *adyton* – the secret chamber of oracle-giving in the temple of Apollo at Delphi, – the priestess seated on top of her tripod stool, a shallow bowl of spring water in one hand and a twig of laurel leaves in the other, while she inhales the fumes swirling up from a fissure in the ground. She mouths words as the male priests lean in to listen, while the following is heard spoken by Socrates:] that *no one was wiser*.

[Cut to a view of the jury seating area as seen from the speaker's platform. Jurors break out into shouts and angry gestures throughout the crowd. Some yell heresy; others yell hearsay; and others, dressed in the earthier-hued *chitons*, yell out earthier expressions. Cut to Socrates, firmly planted at the center of the platform, nodding his head. Cut next to the herald as he stands up and turns around to address the jurors and spectators. He demands that all lower their voices and keep their silence. A juror shouts back that they cannot keep quiet at such impiety. Many others shout out in agreement with him. The herald continues to demand for there to be order in the court. The shouts and out-

27

rage take several more moments to subside. Cut back to Socrates as relative calm retakes the courtroom. He points his hand at the bench for the defense.]

His brother here will now act as a witness for him and for what he said, since Chaerephon himself has passed away.

[Socrates moves to the side of the *bēma* closest to the prosecution bench. Chaerecrates, a man in his sixties, rises from the defense bench and approaches the platform. Cut to the court clerk as he dips his reed quill into the inkwell and smoothes out a sheet of papyrus on the writing table in front of him. Cut next to the juror in charge of the *clepsydra* as he plugs the copper spout in order to keep the testimony off of the defendant's time. Cut back to Chaerecrates, at the center of the speaker's platform as he begins by stating his name, his home district and that he is the younger brother of Chaerephon. The court magistrate asks Chaerecrates to swear to the truth of his testimony by Zeus, Demeter, and Poseidon, which he promptly does. He then reports how Chaerephon did indeed go to the oracle at Delphi and ask if anyone were wiser than Socrates, and the answer was *no*. The jurors remain subdued, though constantly commenting among themselves in undertones and whisperings. The magistrate instructs Chaerecrates to come to the clerk's table in order to sign his testimony. Chaerecrates descends the three steps of the *bēma* as Socrates moves back to its center. Cut to a close-up of the copper spout of the water-clock as the plug is removed and time is again allowed to flow. Cut back to the view of Socrates alone on the *bēma*.]

Understand why I have just related this account to you: I am about to provide a detailed explanation of how the barrage of attacks on me had its origin. After hearing Chaerephon's report, I took it to heart and thought it over in this way: "What on earth does the god mean, and what type of riddle is this? I am not aware of myself being wise in any way. What can he possibly mean, then, by proclaiming that I am the wisest man? He most certainly cannot be lying – that would be against divine law." And for the longest time I was puzzled and at a complete loss for what he could have meant. But then, in order to prove him right or wrong – and I did this with *great reluctance*, I must say – I set off on the following investigation.

[Cut to the court clerk as he uses the blotting cloth on the freshly-inscribed papyrus. He dips the reed quill into the inkwell again and hands it to Chaerecrates. Chaerecrates grasps the quill as he leans over to sign the document. Cut back to Socrates on the platform.]

I went straight to a man who is well-known for his wisdom so that right then and there – if anywhere – I could refute the oracle and declare to its giver: "This man here is wiser than I am, but you proclaimed that *I* should be the wiser." So I questioned and examined him … [A juror shouts out who?] … – a man whose name I would rather not say, Athenians, since it was one of our public men I was speaking with who made this impression on me. … [Socrates glances briefly at the bench for the prosecution. Cut to a close-up of Anytus's face.]

[Cut from the real-time of the courtroom. Flashback to a scene at Anytus's home many years earlier. The setting is the *andrōnitis*, the room in the household used for entertaining male guests. Socrates, Anytus, a young man named Meno and several others are gathered there. Some of them are reclining, some are sitting upright on the *clinēs* – the cushioned bedsteads, in this case ornately-decorated with the shapes of animal paws carved at the foot of each wooden leg. They are engaging in a symposium – a drinking party – with drinking cups and food spread out on a low-rising table at the center. A handful of Anytus's slaves are stationed at different places in the room, waiting for their commands. Socrates is in the process of asking Anytus if Meno should seek out the tutorship of one of the sophists in order to be instructed on how to be virtuous in such matters as household economy or running city affairs. Anytus reacts with shock at the suggestion, stating that sophists are harmful men who bring nothing but corruption and ruin to those who listen to them. Socrates asks how is it, then, that Protagoras, the most-renowned sophist, could teach for forty years if his instruction brought such calamities to his pupils? Anytus places the blame for this lack of retribution on the pupils themselves and their family members who allowed them to be taught by such a man. Socrates asks if a sophist has somehow wronged Anytus; and if not, why is he so hard on them? Anytus explains that he has never known or spoken to any sophist and never will. Socrates inquires how it is, then, that Anytus can make such accusations against sophists without any personal experience of them. Anytus claims that what he has heard of them is enough. So who *can* teach virtue, Socrates asks, if the sophists cannot? Anytus replies that any decent Athenian citizen can do a sufficient job of that. Socrates asks why it is, then, that virtuous men do not have virtuous sons – is it because they refuse to teach their virtues to them? Socrates glances at Anytus's son, who has been seated on a *cline* against a far wall, observing the interaction with a respectful silence. His son is a young man who, instead of following in his father's footsteps as a public man, has remained in the traditional profession of his family – that of a tanner, working animal hides into leather. Socrates, with a gleam in his eyes, looks back at Anytus and asserts that *virtue can certainly not be taught.* Cut back to the real-time of the courtroom and Socrates on the speaker's platform.]

While we were talking together I realized that even though this was a man who appeared wise to many other people, and especially *to himself,* in fact he was not. And when I tried to make him aware of this – that even though he might believe himself to be wise, that may not be the case, – at that moment he became enraged and began to hate me, as did many of the on-lookers who were there.

[Cut from the real-time of the courtroom back to the *andrōnītis.* Anytus, with a look of hurt pride on his face, is standing next to the *clinē* on which he had been seated. He criticizes Socrates sharply for speaking badly of people too easily and warns him that he had better be more careful and watch himself. Close-up of the foreboding look on Anytus's face. Cut back to real-time and Socrates on the *bēma.*]

I walked away from this encounter thinking to myself: "I have more wisdom than *that* man, at least, but probably neither one of us has any type of true or worthy knowledge. Unlike me, though, he believes that he *does* know the truth about certain things even if he really does not. But me, well aware that I do not have such knowledge, *I do not believe that I do.* I seem, then, to have a slight advantage over him in just this respect: that whatever I do not know, *I do not believe myself to know.*"

[Socrates looks around the courtroom, examining the faces. Cut to a sector of jurors as several of their heads bob up and down in agreement with his last statement. Most of them, however, appear unaffected. Cut back to Socrates on the *bēma.*]

After this first attempt to disprove the oracle – and because of my failure to do so, – I sought out another politician, one who was considered to be even wiser than the first man I examined, and the situation seemed to *completely repeat itself*, with me once again becoming despised by the man I questioned and by many of those who were listening to us. But I nonetheless continued my investigation, going from one man to another, with growing agony and alarm at how I was making myself more and more hated – but I felt an overwhelming obligation to devote myself to what concerned Apollo. It was my duty to go about in search of what his oracle meant and to question all of those who seemed to have any type of knowledge. And, by the Dog, Athenians … [Visual of Anubis, the jackal-headed god in Egypt; then cut to the faces of the men seated on the bench for the defense as a few of them grin. Return to the view of the *bēma*.] … – and by necessity that the truth be spoken here, – I swear that this was what I discovered: nearly all of the men who had the best reputations for wisdom appeared to be in need of wisdom *the most*, while men of much lower standing were actually far more keen and sensible when it came to being wise in some sense.

[Socrates pauses as his eyes are pulled downward. Cut to the herald as he slides two more wooden rings across the horizontal pole, making a total of four rings at that end of the device. Return to Socrates, lifting his gaze.]

Really I must go into greater detail of all of the turmoil and trouble I went through in my search for the truth – I labored so painstakingly to prove to myself that the oracle was, in fact, *irrefutable*.

[A few gruff mumblings of disbelief emanate from the courtroom. Socrates glances around searchingly before continuing in a calm and well-measured voice.]

After questioning the politicians, I went next to the poets – the men who write tragedies and choral hymns and in other styles – so I could see in what ways they were wiser than me and catch myself red-handed in my ignorance. I brought along their poems – the ones that seemed most carefully-crafted to me – and would ask them what they meant, so that I might learn something from them at the same time. And it pains me to tell you what I learned, Athenians, but the truth must be spoken. Nearly every one of the men who were gathered around and listening to me and the poet I was conversing with, most of *them* could have spoken better and with more insight about the very things *the poets themselves had created*. It did not take me long to realize that poets do not create what they create by way of any type of wisdom but through some type of inner nature and divine inspiration – just like those who give us prophecies and oracles. The seers and prophets say many valuable and important things, but they do not comprehend the meaning of the words they speak. Clearly this is the same type of experience that the poets go through when the gods inspire them and they compose their works. I also discovered that, on account of their poetic gifts, the poets considered themselves to have a great knowledge of many matters *other than poetry*, … [His face contorts into a look of distaste.] … matters which they knew *little or nothing about*. … [He relaxes his facial features and nods his head.] … The end result was, as I walked away from this part of my inquiry, I was certain that I had the same advantage over the poets as I had over the politicians.

[Cut to a section of jurymen, several of whom are watching Socrates with rapt attention. Several others, however, appear agitated and impatient. Cut back to the *bēma*.]

The final leg of my investigation led me to the craftsmen and artisans. I knew practically nothing of their crafts and skills, so

I was confident I would discover them to have a wealth of valuable knowledge. And in this I was not disappointed. They had knowledge that I did not have, and in that regard they were wiser than me. … [His face again tenses up into a look of distaste.] … But even the noble craftspeople, Athenians, clung to the same false notion as the poets did, believing themselves to be overly wise when it came to other matters of great importance – far beyond their works and crafts – because of their professional expertise. And it was this error of theirs, I believe, that kept any greater wisdom out of their grasp and hidden away from them. So I had to ask myself, with the oracle in mind: "If I were given the choice, which way would I rather be: as I currently am, not wise in the ways that they are wise but not ignorant in the way that they are ignorant; or *as* they are, with both of their particular types of wisdom and ignorance?" The answer I gave – to myself and the oracle – … [He opens his palm and places it on the coarse fabric of the dirt-gray cloak wrapped across his chest.] … was that I was much better off *as I am*.

> [Socrates relaxes his arm and stares out at the jury. Cut to a sector of jurymen whose faces contain an equal mixture of skeptical, favorable, and unaffected expressions. Cut back to Socrates as a troubled look takes shape on his face.]

Due to this investigation – these inquiries spurred on by the god, Athenians, – I have a great deal of animosity working against me, and of a most difficult and severe kind. It has stirred up all sorts of ill-repute and attacks on me – all on account of being labeled "wise" by the oracle and by the men who mistakenly believe that I know the truth about whatever I am able to refute in others. But the reality is that *the gods alone* are truly wise, and what was meant by the oracle was that human wisdom is of little or no worth, … [Socrates lifts his palm and folds back his fingers so that they are directed at himself.] ... Apollo mentioning this man Socrates – the god apparently using me and my name as an example – as if to say: "The wisest among men are those who know – like Socrates – that no mortal is, in truth, worthy of the highest wisdom." ... [He lowers his arm.] ... This is why I have been wandering around until the present day examining and scrutinizing Athenians and non-Athenians alike: to see if I can find someone who *is* truly wise, someone with any type of true or worthy knowledge. And whenever I prove to a man that he does not, in fact, possess the wisdom he believes himself to possess, *I am acting in defense of Apollo.*

[A number of exasperated and skeptical groans are released. One man loudly grumbles how impious all of this is. Another man complains that this is nothing but sheer madness. Socrates calmly continues, without concern for their remarks.]

And as a result of all of this – of these never-ending labors – I have had time to do nothing worth mentioning in public affairs, let alone those of my own, and have lived in constant poverty due to my devotion to the god.

[Cut to a view of the prosecution bench, displaying Anytus in his gilt-embroidered indigo *chiton* seated between Meletus and Lycon, both of them dressed in their clean white *chitons*. All three of them are sporting high-quality sandals. Cut back to Socrates in his gray-soot clothing, standing barefoot on the *bēma*.]

And what adds to my notoriety, young men choose to gather around me, the ones who take pleasure in seeing men being examined. These are the young men with the most free time ... [Cut to the bench for the defense and a close-up of one of the young men, the one who has broad shoulders and a penetrating gaze, while the following is heard spoken:] – mostly the sons of the wealthy [Cut back to Socrates on the platform.] ... – and after observing my questioning they often go off and try to imitate me by examining other men on their own. When they do this they discover that there are, indeed, a great many men who believe themselves to know a great many things which, in reality, they know little or nothing about. And if this lack of genuine knowledge is made clear to them through a few questions and answers, they get enraged at *me* – not at themselves – and curse me with: "Socrates is a most vile and despicable man who is corrupting the minds and morals of our youth!" But when someone asks them what it is I do exactly that is so awful, and what it is that I teach, they have nothing to say *because they do not know*. In order, though, not to appear to be at a loss, they reply with the usual ready-made accusations against all philosophers, such as "things in the sky and beneath the earth" and "does not believe in the gods" and "makes the weaker argument stronger." I think the truth is that they would not like to admit that they have been exposed as pretending to have knowledge that they do not actually have. And since these men are so concerned with their honor and reputation and get so angry – so many of them railing against me in a way that exerts so much influence over others, – they have been able to fill your ears for far too many years with their hostile criticisms and lies. And on the strength of this ... [Socrates waves an arm toward his present accusers.] ... Meletus now sets against me, with Lycon and Anytus at his side ... [Socrates steps over to their side of the *bēma* and points his hand at them. Cut to a close-up of the young man with shoulder-length limp hair and the hawk-like nose and eyes.] ... – Meletus, expressing outrage for the poets; ... [Cut to a close-up of the other young man, who has hair like that of a statue, finely-styled and not a single strand out of place.] ... Lycon, for the orators of the Assembly; ... [Cut to a close-up of the proud-faced older man, the champion of Athenian democracy.] ... and Anytus, for the craftsmen and statesmen. ... [Return to Socrates on the *bēma* as he looks back at the jury.] ... So

36

I would certainly be astonished if, as I said at the start, I could remove this prejudice and bias from you – as gigantic as it has become – in the short amount of time I am given here.

[Cut to a close-up of the *clepsydra*, with the thin stream of water spurting out from the copper spout of the upper jar into the lower jar. Cut back to the *bēma* and Socrates standing at the center of it, nodding his head conclusively.]

And there you have it, Athenians, all of the truth. I have hidden nothing from you and have held nothing back – and I am certainly not ignorant of the fact that I am an object of public scorn *because of* this very characteristic of mine to speak so openly and honestly. This in itself ought to serve as an indication, if not *proof*, that what I say is true and that these are truly the reasons for the widespread ill-repute and attacks against me. And whether you take this matter up here and now or again anytime later, you will find it to be exactly as I have just described it to you.

[Socrates comes to a stop and stands motionless on the speaker's platform. He stares blankly in front of himself for several moments; then with a sudden blink the shine returns to his eyes.]

Defense Against
the Recent Charges

Socrates

As for my first accusers and their accusations, that should serve as an adequate defense for your purpose here today. I will now take on the task of defending myself against the noble and patriotic Meletus ... [Socrates tilts his head toward the bench for the prosecution.] ... – as *he* describes himself – and my more recent accusers. And being, as they are, a different set of accusers, let's bring up their different set of accusations. They swore under oath something to this effect: "Socrates is guilty of crimes against the state. He is a bad and corrupting influence on the young, and he does not believe in the gods worshipped by the city but in other new and unknown things in the spirit world."

> [Socrates pauses and contemplates the last phrase. A look of bewilderment takes shape on his face. After a moment he regains his composure and continues.]

Such are the charges. Now let's examine them one by one. First of all it states that I commit a crime by being a bad influence on the young – but, Athenians, I tell you that *Meletus* is the one who is committing a crime. He recklessly drags men into court on baseless grounds ... [Visual of the same courtroom a few months prior to Socrates' trial, with a view of the *bēma* and the benches for the litigants. Meletus is seated on the bench for the prosecution; a man named Andocides is speaking on the platform, defending himself against a charge of impiety for profaning the Eleusinian mysteries. Cut to Meletus – his beaked face tense with righteousness – seated at the side of two men who have joined him in the prosecution of Andocides, as the following is heard spoken by Socrates:] while pretending to take them seriously and be highly concerned when in fact he cares *nothing whatever about them*. [Cut from Meletus a few months ago to Meletus now, seated at the side of Anytus and Lycon, his beaked face again tense with righteousness. Cut back to Socrates on the *bēma*.] ... This is all a childish game to him that he plays with a deep look of concern on his face.

[A jury member shouts out – in a raspy voice – that this is no game, Socrates. A handful of others shout out in support of the sentiment. Socrates glares at the area of the jury where he believes the shout came from.]

This is *indeed* the reality of the situation, and I will now attempt to provide you with proof. ... [He walks to the side of the *bēma* closest to the prosecution and points his hand at the platform.] ... Come now, Meletus, stand here and speak.

[Cut to Meletus, who remains seated, eyes full of rage. After a few moments, a juror shouts out for him to stand and speak. Several others then echo him. Cut to the magistrate as he announces that the accuser will arise and respond to the defendant's questions. Cut back to Meletus, as he reluctantly rises up and mounts the three steps of the *bēma*. Return to a view of the *bēma* as Socrates moves to the opposite side of it from Meletus. The two of them stand motionless for a moment, two meters apart, staring at each other. Meletus, with great agitation, then turns away from Socrates and directs his gaze at the courtroom. Socrates keeps his eyes focused on his opponent. He begins the cross-examination in a gentle manner.]

You consider it to be of the utmost importance that our young men are molded into being as good and virtuous as possible – correct?

Meletus

[Proudly:] I do.

Socrates

Tell us, then: who is it that does this? Who molds them into better condition? You obviously must know the answer, considering how much of a concern it is to you. You have exposed one man who, as you claim, corrupts them – and bring me here before these men on that accusation, – so you certainly should speak now and inform us who it is that *makes them better*.

> [Meletus turns his head and glares suspiciously at Socrates. Socrates, his large eyes gleaming, waits for several moments.]

See how you are silent, Meletus, and have nothing to say? Doesn't that seem shameful to you and serve as proof of what I maintain, that you care nothing about the grounds of your charges against me?

> [Meletus scowls and turns his head back to the jury area. Socrates waits for a few moments, observing Meletus carefully, before continuing in a friendly tone.]

Come now, be so good as to tell us: who can make them better?

Meletus

[Stated simply:] The laws.

Socrates

But that is not what I am asking you, my good friend. What *person* – who is already well aware of the laws – can make them better?

Meletus

[Sweeping an arm across the expanse of the room:] These men, Socrates. The jury members.

Socrates

What do you mean, Meletus? These men here are capable of instructing the young and improving their moral integrity?

Meletus

Absolutely.

Socrates

All of them? Or some of them can, some of them cannot?

Meletus

All of them.

Socrates

[Smiling brightly:] Praise to Hera, that certainly *is* good news. What an abundance of benefactors the youth of our city have.

[Several laughs spurt out from the crowd. Meletus glares huntingly for the perpetrators. After a moment,

Socrates continues in a gentle tone.]

But then, who else? How about these people listening in ... [He extends his arm to indicate the area up and at the back of the courtroom. Cut to a view of the standing-room only crowd of men separated from the jury seating area by a wooden railing – a couple dozen of them spilling out onto the uppermost steps against the walls, – while the following is heard spoken:] – the spectators in the court [Cut back to the *bēma*.] ... – do they improve the young as well, or not?

Meletus

They do too.

Socrates

[After careful consideration:] And what about the members of the Council of Five Hundred?

Meletus

They do as well.

Socrates

[With a tilt of his head:] Could it be the case, then, that those who partake in the Assembly – every Athenian male who can vote – could corrupt the youth? Or does each one of them have a positive influence on the young too?

Meletus

Each of them does too.

Socrates

[With slight shock:] It seems as though every Athenian makes our youth more noble and praiseworthy – *except for me*. I alone seem to corrupt them. Is this what you are saying?

Meletus

That is exactly what I say.

Socrates

[Assuming a look of gravitas:] You curse me to great misfortune, in that case.

> [Cut to the herald. He slides two more wooden rings from one end of the horizontal pole to the other. Cut back to Socrates – who has failed to notice – as his gravitas transforms into a look of inquisitiveness.]

But tell me this: do you think it is true for horses as well, that nearly every man is good for them and makes them better, with just one man who makes them worse? ... [Meletus turns his head and glares suspiciously at Socrates again.] ... Or is the complete opposite the truth: that only one man is capable of grooming them into excellent condition – or better yet, very few men, like the professional horse-trainers, – while all other men who deal with horses worsen the chance of that excellence ever being achieved? ... [Meletus continues to glare at him.] ... Isn't this the case, Meletus, that only a small number of men are actually capable of improving horses, or any other animal for that matter?

> [Meletus twists his head to look at the bench for the prosecution. Cut to Anytus, who responds to his

glance with a shake of his head: a warning not to get tangled and trapped in this style of questioning. Cut back to the platform as Meletus turns his head from Anytus to the jury members, a mixture of suspicion and rage on his face. Socrates continues, eyes fixed on his opponent.]

It most certainly *is*, whether you or Anytus admit it or not. What boundless joy we would have for the young if just *one man alone* were out to harm them while all of the rest did whatever they could for their benefit. ... [Socrates intensifies into scorn.] ... Meletus, you expose your utter lack of consideration and concern for the young too clearly. You care nothing at all about the charges that bring me here today.

[Cut to the bench for the prosecution as Anytus stands up and turns toward the court magistrate. He states that he objects to this style of questioning, a style so full of tricks and traps. Cut next to the bench for the defense as Chaerecrates stands up. He informs the magistrate that this style is Socrates' customary style, which he has already begged the court to allow him. Cut to the magistrate, seated between the herald and court clerk, as he considers the two statements. During the pause, a variety of shouts are heard from the jurors and spectators. One man calls out that Socrates has every right to speak in his usual manner; another man calls out that such trickery has no place in a court of law; and one spectator at the far back shouts out that Socrates is *making the weaker argument stronger* – which is immediately followed by laughter and a general commotion. During the uproar, the magistrate speaks something to the herald, who then stands up, turns around and announces that the defendant's style of questioning will be allowed. A mixture of jeers and cheers result, after which the mass of men settles down. Cut back to Socrates and Meletus on the *bēma*.]

Socrates

Tell us, then, Meletus – with Zeus as our witness, – which do you think is better: to live among citizens who are good and virtuous or among those who are bad and vile?

[Meletus ignores the question, staring forward at the court magistrate, barely able to contain his anger at his decision. Socrates waits a moment before continuing.]

Come now, my friend, answer up. I am asking you nothing difficult. Bad people treat those close to them in a bad way, while good people treat them in a good way – isn't this the case?

Meletus

[With contempt:] Of course it is.

Socrates

And is there anyone who likes to be treated in a bad way and be harmed by those around him rather than treated in a good way and be helped? … [Meletus continues glaring forward.] … Keep answering, my good friend: the law requires that you respond. Is there anyone who *likes to be harmed*?

Meletus

[With continued contempt:] Certainly not.

Socrates

And today you bring me to this court for corrupting the young and worsening their well-being – which I do willingly or unwillingly?

Meletus

Willingly, of course.

Socrates

[With shock:] How can that be, Meletus? Are you so much wiser than me – you at your age and me at mine – that you are cognizant of the fact that bad people do bad things to those who are around them, but I have become so grossly ignorant that I do *not* recognize this fact? And can it also be that I do not recognize that if I do something wrong to someone close to me, I run the risk of receiving his vengeance in return – *and*, as you suggest, I would *willingly* carry out that wrongful act? ... [The expression on Socrates' face transforms from one of shock into one of rebuke.] ... I do not believe this, Meletus – as, I am sure, no other man does. Either I do not corrupt the young or, if I do, I do so *unwillingly*, which makes you wrong on both accounts. And if I do corrupt the young unwillingly, the law does not bring me here to a public court for such a mistake. I ought to be taken aside privately in that case to be informed and warned about my actions. Certainly if I knew better, I would stop doing what I do unintentionally. ... [Socrates speaks in his most reproachful tone yet.] ... But you did not want to do this. You avoided meeting with me in private and informing me about what I was doing wrong – bringing me here, instead, where the law brings people who need punishment, not instruction.

[Several shouts of favor burst out from the courtroom. Meletus scornfully scans the crowd. Socrates turns toward the jury.]

Athenians, what I claimed before is clear by now, that our youth have been of no concern whatsoever to Meletus. ... [Socrates turns back to his youthful opponent and speaks in a tone full of scrutiny.] ... But still, tell us: how do you think I corrupt the young, Meletus? Or is it obvious that – as you suggest in your charges against me – I teach them not to pay heed to the gods that the city worships but to other new things in the spirit world not recognized by the state?

[Socrates waits for a response. None is given.]

Isn't that what you mean, that I weaken the moral and patriotic fiber of the young by teaching them this?

Meletus

[Forcefully:] That is exactly what I mean.

Socrates

For the sake of the gods, Meletus – the very beings we are now discussing, – clarify something for me and these men here. I cannot figure out whether you mean that I encourage the young to believe in *some* gods – not, though, the gods of Athens, but in others, and this is what you are accusing me of ... [Socrates momentarily assumes a gentler tone.] ... – since if you are, that means I *do* believe there are gods and am not entirely godless or guilty of anything in that respect, ... [The scrutiny returns.] ... – or are you suggesting that I do not believe in *any gods at all*, and this is what I teach to others?

Meletus

[Turning his head to look directly at Socrates:] That is what I mean, that you do not believe in any gods at all.

Socrates

You amaze me, Meletus. How can you say that? Don't I believe that the sun and the moon are gods, just as others do?

Meletus

[Turning toward the jury:] By Zeus, jurymen, he does not! He says that the sun is a stone, and the moon is made of earth.

Socrates

Who do you think I am, my dear Meletus – *Anaxagoras*? ... [Visual of the philosopher Anaxagoras with the statesman Pericles, a papyrus spread out in front of them on a table, displaying a diagram of the theory that moonlight is a reflection of light from the sun, while the following is heard spoken:] Do you think so little of these men here, so poorly-educated they are, that they do not know that the books of Anaxagoras are filled with such theories? [Visuals of: Anaxagoras being arrested by opponents of Pericles on charges of impiety and atheism; Pericles interceding to secure his release from prison and the death penalty; then Anaxagoras sailing away from the Piraeus – the port of Athens, – being forced into exile, while the following is heard spoken:] And do you really think that young men learn these theories from me, which they can buy at an agora bookstall for a drachma at most, and then have a good laugh at me if I pretend they are my own, especially when they are so outrageous? [Return to Socrates and Meletus on the *bēma*.] ... But in the name of Zeus, do I truly seem to you to believe there are no gods at all?

Meletus

By Zeus, you do not believe in them at all.

Socrates

[Full of scorn:] You cannot be taken seriously, Meletus – in particular, as it seems, not even *by yourself.* ... [Socrates turns to address the jury. He points his hand at Meletus.] ... This man, Athenians, is a most impudent and insolent man who cannot control himself. His charges were brought against me entirely out of some type of arrogant rage and the inability to restrain it, let alone his youthfulness. ... [Meletus scowls intensely.] ... If anything, he appears right now to be trying out a ruse on us that he concocted for the occasion: "Will Socrates the Wise figure out that this is all a game to me – which I play by making conflicting statements – or will I deceive him and the others who are listening?" He blatantly contradicts one of his very own accusations against me, as if it has become: "Socrates is guilty of not believing in the gods, *while believing in the gods.*" This is nothing but a childish prank.

> [A man in the crowd shouts out that this is *not* a prank; another man calls out for Socrates to explain himself; one man, exasperated, shouts for Socrates to simply get to the point. Socrates holds up his palm.]

Men of Athens, follow my reasoning closely now as to why he appears to me to speak this way. ... [He turns his head toward the tense young man.] ... You, Meletus, provide us with answers. ... [He returns his gaze to his judges.] ... And as for the rest of you – as I begged of you at the start, – bear in mind not to interrupt me with any type of outcry if I make my argument in my usual manner. ... [Socrates redirects his gaze at Meletus, who continues to glower in the direction of the crowd.] ... Meletus, is there anyone who believes there are matters concerning human beings but who does not believe there *to be* human beings?

[Meletus cannot restrain his rage any longer. He shouts out in protest – to the general mass of men in front of him as much as to the magistrate in particular – that this type of questioning must be forbidden. Many of the jurors and spectators shout out as they did when Anytus made the similar demand: some in support of it, others against it. Socrates turns toward the courtroom and raises his palm. He loudly addresses the crowd.]

Men of Athens, let him respond.

[Cut to the view from the back rows of the jury area as the herald stands up, faces the jurors, raises both of his palms and demands for there to be silence. He stands in that position for several moments until the commotion begins to subside. Cut back to the *bēma* as Socrates turns toward Meletus.]

And may he stop himself from shouting out like that again.

[The courtroom settles down into its usual background din of mumblings and whisperings. Socrates continues his questioning in a philosophic tone.]

Is there anyone who does not believe there to be horses but who *does* believe there are matters *concerning horses*? ... [Meletus is silent.] ... Or anyone who does not believe there to be flute players but who *does* believe there are matters *concerning flute playing*? ... [Meletus remains silent.] ... No, there is no

one like that, my fine young man – and unless you care to reply to my questions, I will continue to reply on your behalf to
the jurymen here.

[Socrates pauses in order to scrutinize the tension and
rage of his youthful opponent. Meletus stands rigidly
staring straight ahead, fists clenched. After a few moments, Socrates continues.]

At the very least, answer this next one: is there anyone who
believes there are *matters* in the spirit world but who does not
believe there to be *beings* in the spirit world?

Meletus

[With slight hesitation:] No, there is not.

Socrates

[His face brightening:] How kind of you to reply – though a
bit reluctantly – as your presence in this courtroom requires of
you. ... [His bright tone quickly transits into one of intent seriousness.] ... You said in your speech that I teach about and
believe in things in the spirit world, whether of a new kind or
old. In any case, I believe in spirit-like things of some sort according to your own charge against me – which, I will remind
you, you swore to under oath. ... [Socrates intensifies his
tone.] ... If I believe in *things* in the spirit world, then surely I
must believe in *beings* in the spirit world – isn't that the case?

[Meletus remains rigidly poised, the wrath in his eyes
directed straight ahead. Socrates waits several moments before continuing.]

It most certainly *is*, and I take your silence to mean that we

51

agree. And don't we also agree that these beings are gods or, at the very least, the children of gods?

[Meletus continues to glare forward, tight-fisted. After a few moments of carefully inspecting him, Socrates presses the point.]

Do we or do we not?

Meletus

[Bitterly:] Of course we do.

Socrates

[Triumphantly:] Well then, if I believe these beings exist – as we agree, – and if they are gods of some sort, this would explain what I meant when I said you are playing a prank on us like a childish game. You said that I did not believe in any gods but then that I *do*, since I believe there are things and beings in the spirit world. And if it happens that these beings are only the *children* of gods – some born out of wedlock, or from nymphs, or from other mothers as some people think, – what man could believe there to be *children* of gods but not *gods themselves*? It would be just as ridiculous as to believe there were offspring from the coupling of horses and donkeys – the half-breed mules – but not believe there to be either horses or donkeys.

[Cut to a sector of jurors. Several of them are grinning. Cut back to the *bēma*.]

Meletus, it can only be that you are testing these charges out on me because you are at a complete loss of any true act of injustice you can accuse me of committing. ... [Socrates turns away from Meletus and directs his words at the courtroom.] … How could you persuade anyone with the dimmest of minds that one and the same person could believe in things in the spirit world and matters of a divine kind but *not* believe there to be beings in the spirit world or gods or the heroic demi-gods for that matter? *It cannot be done.*

[Cut to a view of the *bēma* with both benches at its sides. Socrates points his hand at the bench for the prosecution and tells Meletus that he may now sit down. Meletus breaks his forward-fixed glare and turns his head to give Socrates one last spiteful look before descending the platform. He takes his seat at the side of Anytus, and the three of them – Meletus, Anytus and Lycon – immediately break into a discussion in undertones. Socrates moves to the center of the platform, watching them whisper. He then takes a few steps toward their side of the *bēma* and eyes Anytus very carefully. The magistrate asks if the defendant will call up another of the accusers for cross-examination. The three accusers become mute and return Socrates' stare. Anytus, proud-faced, places his hands on his thighs – on the rich indigo fabric of his *chiton*, – readying himself to rise up. For the first time since Meletus took the stand the trickle from the *clepsydra* can faintly be heard again. After several moments, Socrates turns and slowly steps back to the center of the speaker's platform.]

As for the charges Meletus has brought against me, Athenians, what I have said so far should be more than enough. I am *not* guilty of any crimes as he alleges, and I see no need of going on any further with this part of my defense. … [Socrates glances earnestly around the courtroom.] … But do understand the truth of what I told you before, that a great amount of animosity has grown against me in the hearts of a great amount of people. And this animosity – this *overgrown hatred* – is what brings me here and condemns me today, if anything does … [He sweeps his arm toward the prosecution.] … – not Meletus or Anytus, but the vicious lies and resentment of a great many people. … [He slowly nods his head.] … Hard feelings such as these have condemned many other decent and innocent men, and I am sure they will continue to do so. There is no fear of that stopping here with me.

[Socrates pauses with a look of solemnity on his face. Cut to the corner with the water-clock as the allotted juryman is refilling the upper jar. Cut next to the herald, who slides two more wooden rings along the horizontal pole of his contraption, disrupting the balance of six rings at both ends into eight at one end and four at the other. Cut back to the *bēma*.]

Digression on Socrates' Life

Socrates

Now perhaps someone here might ask: "Don't you have the least bit of regret, Socrates, for pursuing a course in life that has brought you now to the brink of the punishment of death?" I would be quite right to answer this with: "You have it all wrong, my good man, if you think that any of us – any of us of even the *least bit of worth* – must take the risk of living or dying into consideration whenever we set out on a course of action. The only thing we ever need to consider is whether or not we are doing something *right or wrong*, or whether we are performing the actions of a *good man or bad*. According to your reasoning, the heroic demi-gods who died at Troy must have been worth very little – in particular the son of the sea-goddess Thetis.

[Cut to an image of Achilles and Hector confronting each other outside the walls of Troy, clutching their swords and shields and locked in a hostile stare. Cut back to Socrates on the speaker's platform, with the most serious expression yet on his face.]

He had such a low regard for the danger of death – faced with the prospect of lifelong disgrace if he did not kill Hector, an act his wrath was raging to do – that when his mother revealed a prophesy to him by saying: 'My son, if you do avenge the slaying of your beloved friend Patroclus and succeed in slaying Hector, *you yourself shall die*, for your fate is instantly determined upon Hector's demise.' – Even after hearing this, Achilles *still* thought little of the dangers that lay in wait for him, fearing far more a dishonorable life and not avenging his friend. He answered his mother: ... [In the lofty tone reserved for quoting scripture.] ... 'Instantly, then, I wish to die once I have meted out justice on the wrong-doer's head, since I could not stand to remain here, ridiculed next to the curved bows of the ships, a burden to the land.' ... [Socrates glares at the jury members.] ... Do you think that he had the least bit of concern for danger and death in this decision?"

[Cut to an area of jurymen, several of whom have devout and deeply-moved expressions on their faces. Most of the others, however, appear hardly affected at all. Cut back to Socrates.]

The truth of the matter, Athenians, is that wherever someone stations himself in life, believing that place to be the most auspicious for his plans and purposes – or wherever he *becomes* stationed by a commander above, – it is there that he must

55

stand his ground and face the onslaughts of life, always on the look-out for unwise words or deeds that may lead him into disgrace and dishonor. No other misfortune, *not even death*, is worse. ... [Visual of Socrates during the Peloponnesian War, middle-aged, clad in the armor of a hoplite soldier – a spear in one hand and a circular shield in the other, – marching forward in a phalanx of Athenian soldiers as they approach a Spartan phalanx, while the following is heard spoken:] Athenians, what great disgrace and dishonor I would have brought on myself if – when I was stationed in the war against Sparta by our commanders, the very generals you elected to lead us in Poteidaia and Amphipolis and at the temple in Delium [Return to Socrates on the *bēma*] ... – if, while I was where those men stationed me, standing my ground and risking my life just as everyone else who was there, I had abandoned my post. ... [Visuals of: Chaerophon being told the oracle at Delphi by a temple priest; Chaerophon reporting the oracle to Socrates; then Socrates in an animated discussion with a small group of men near the money-changers' area of the agora, while the following is heard spoken:] Or if – when Apollo had stationed me *in my course of life*, which is how I have always looked at the oracle, understanding my god-given task to be a life of philosophy, of examining myself and others [Cut back to the *bēma*] ... – if at *that* point, out of fear of death or anything else, I had abandoned my post. How shameful and virtueless of me that would have been, and how truly I could have been brought to trial for not believing there to be any gods, since I was paying no heed to the oracle and fearing death and thinking myself wise when I most certainly was not.

[Socrates takes a moment to scan the faces in front of him, a pensive expression on his face. He then resumes in his most philosophical tone.]

To have a fear of death, Athenians, only *seems* to be wise when in fact it is not, since it is pretending to know something *that is not known*. Nobody knows death, or even if it happens to be the greatest of all blessings to man – but everyone fears it as if perfectly sure it is the *greatest of all curses*. And how can this type of ignorance – believing to have certain knowledge about something unknown – not be deserving of the utmost scorn and reproach? Without a doubt I differ from most other men in this regard. In fact, if I were to claim myself to be wiser in some respect than another man, it would be in this: I have *no certain knowledge* about what happens in the House of Hades – I do not know what happens after death, – and I am *aware* that I know nothing certain about it.

[Socrates stops and stares out at the crowd, allowing the weight of his words to thoroughly sink in. He then nods his head.]

But something I *do* know is that not acting justly and not paying heed to those who are your superiors – whether man or god – *is* shameful and wrong.

[Cut to the bench for the defense as the eyes of the young broad-shouldered man brighten at hearing Socrates make a rare statement of positive knowledge. Cut back to Socrates.]

Unlike acts such as these, though – ones that I know to be bad, – I will never fear or flee from anything that, for all I really do know, might be good. And because of this, even if you let me go today, … [Visual of Anytus earlier this same morning, standing on the *bēma*, with Lycon and Meletus seated on the wooden bench at the back of the platform against the wall, informing the court that Socrates had the option of self-exile but refused to take it, while the following is heard spoken:] even if you did not agree with what Anytus said in his remarks, that I did not have to come here today, but since I did come you have no choice now but to sentence me to death, [Cut back to Socrates as he motions his arm toward the doorway near the *clepsydra*.] ... because if you do not and I am allowed to leave freely with my life, all of your sons who learn from Socrates and act upon his words will utterly ruin themselves. Even if Anytus failed to persuade you with these words, and you were to say to me: "At this point, Socrates, we are not going to side with Anytus but will let you go on this one condition: that you give up your life of philosophy and put an end to the examination and scrutiny of others. If you are caught doing this again, then you will most certainly meet your death."

[Socrates cautiously casts his gaze up and down the jury member seating area.]

Even if you released me on the terms I just stated, I would say: "Athenians, I appreciate your kind gesture and am filled with affection, but I will indeed pay heed to the god Apollo rather than to you. ... [He places his palm over the portion of his light-gray cloak that is wrapped across his chest.] ... As long as I live and breathe, I will never stop my life of philosophy – my search for truth and wisdom, *divinely-ordained* – and will keep urging and encouraging *you* to seek truth as well, pointing it out to those of you I happen to meet, whenever and wherever it makes itself apparent. ... [Socrates assumes his loftiest tone yet.] ... I will keep goading and coaxing you in my well-known manner, saying: 'My excellent man, being an Athenian as you are – citizen of the city most-famed for the greatness of its strength and wisdom, – aren't you ashamed to be constantly concerned about amassing as much wealth as possible, and high-esteem and public praise, but when it comes to wisdom and truth and amassing as much *excellence of soul* as possible, you lack any such care or concern?'

[Cut to a section of jurors as a few of them scrunch their brows at hearing for the first time the notion that the *psychē* – the soul – rather than the mind is the seat of knowledge and virtue. Return to Socrates, with a look of scrutiny on his face.]

"And if anyone disputes this and insists that he *does* have such virtuous concerns, I will not let him leave me easily, and I will not leave myself, until I have fully questioned him and examined him and proven or disproven him. And if it appears to me that he does not have any virtuous concerns or a genuine care for moral excellence while claiming that he does, I will criticize him for that and tell him that he cares too little about what matters the most in life and too much about what matters the least. … [Socrates nods his head several times.] … I will be like this for any of you I come across – young or old, fellow citizen or foreigner, – but more often for *you*, my fellow Athenians, due to the closeness of our relations. This is, after all, what the god Apollo demands of me, as you are well aware of by now; and no greater good has ever come to you in this city, I say, than my service to the god.

[Several groans and mocking guffaws are released. Socrates remains earnest, speaking from the highest standpoint he can attain.]

"The only reason I have been roaming about Athens and engaging you in discussions has been to persuade you – young and old alike – that your first concern in life ought not to be an enthusiastic concern for your physical needs and personal wealth but an *even more enthusiastic concern for your soul and its perfection*. As I say: 'Virtue does not come from wealth, but *from* virtue comes the possibility of wealth or anything else to be blessings for men, both in personal matters and in matters of state.' … [He gives a tilt to his head.] … And if by saying this I somehow manage to corrupt the young, then somehow it must be harmful. But if anyone claims that I speak otherwise than this – that I am not firmly set on virtue and excellence, –

59

his words are *meaningless*. So with this in mind, Athenians, whether you side with Anytus or not, or whether you let me leave here with my life or not, know fully well that I will never change my ways, *not even if I were to face death again many times over."*

[Socrates pauses and glares defiantly out at the crowd. Room-wide mumblings and grumblings rise up into a commotion. Several jurors and spectators cry out at such unheard of impudence from a man on trial for his life. One man shouts out that this is sheer insolence. Another man cries out that Socrates will face death only once – *here today*. Socrates raises his palm.]

Men of Athens, control yourselves. Keep your voices down and keep with what I requested of you from the start. Do not shout out at what I say and interrupt me but listen closely to my words, since I am certain that listening to me will do you some good.

[He keeps his palm raised until the outburst begins to subside. He then lowers his arm and continues.]

I am about to relate to you further things that could easily cause you to shout out, but by no means do that.

[Socrates pauses and waits for the courtroom to quiet down to its usual din of undertones. Once this is achieved, he continues in a bold voice, his bare feet planted firmly at the center of the *bēma*.]

Athenians, you can rest assured that if you sentence a man like me to death – being, as I say, a servant to goodness and the gods, – you will end up doing far greater harm *to yourselves* than to me. No one – not Meletus, not Anytus – can do me any harm, nor is that even possible. I do not believe that

60

the just workings of the divine allow for a better man to be harmed by a worse man. Perhaps a worse man could kill me or drive me into exile or rob me of my civil rights, but most likely he and others of his ilk consider these penalties to be grave misfortunes, *while I do not.* Much worse to my eyes – and *truly* something grave – is to do what this man here is doing right now, ... [Socrates extends his arm in the direction of Meletus.] ... *trying to have a man unjustly put to death.*

[Cut to the bench for the prosecution. The hawk-like features of Meletus are fiercely focused on their prey. Cut back to Socrates on the *bēma* as he relaxes his arm and again assumes the highest-standing tone he can deliver.]

As things stand, Athenians, I have little need to be making a defense on *my* behalf – as one might think – when there is a far greater need for me to be defending *you* right now in case you make a mistake concerning the gift that the god Apollo has bestowed on you. If you do indeed sentence me to death, you will not have an easy time finding another man of my make, one who is completely devoted to the city and who – though it may sound funny to phrase it this way – has been *stuck to it like a gadfly* by the god. ... [Socrates sticks his index finger into the air.] ... Like a *stinging gadfly* to a brawny and well-bred horse that has become too sluggish and needs a sharp jab to get kicking again. ... [He jabs his index into the air.] ... In just this way and for just this reason, it seems to me, Apollo has latched me onto Athens. I rouse each of you with a jab, sting you with criticism, and prod you into self-improvement. I never cease, crisscrossing the city all day long, setting down wherever anyone will allow. ... [Socrates drops his hand and slowly shakes his head.] ... I tell you, Athenians, there is no other man of my make who will easily come to you – and if you believe this augury of mine, you will spare me here today. But it just might be that you are irritated and angry – like nap-

61

takers who have been pricked awake – and with a single swat you could easily squash me, if Anytus persuades you to do so. You would then have the opportunity to pass the rest of your lives in a mindless slumber – *unless*, that is, Apollo were good enough and concerned enough to send you another man like me. And that I *am* a man such as I have described myself to be – of a kind that has been *divinely bestowed* to the city – what I am about to say may succeed in convincing you.

[Socrates pauses and glances throughout the mass of men in front of him, assuring that he has as much of their undivided attention as he can gather.]

It is not a typical human trait, is it, to have such little concern for my own personal affairs for so many years – including the heartbreak involved in my family being so poorly attended to, – while continuously putting my efforts into *your* affairs, going to each of you on an individual basis with the concern of a father or elder brother in an attempt to convince you to care about virtue and living a just life. If I were profiting in some way from this and taking pay for begging you to better yourselves, then there might be some basic sense to it; but you have seen for yourselves that my accusers … [Cut to the faces of Lycon, Anytus and Meletus staring intently from the prosecution bench, while the following is heard spoken:] – accusing me of everything else they can in such a shameless manner [Return to Socrates.] … – have not been shameless enough to bring forth a witness to claim that I ever took a fee from anyone or ever even asked for one. And I can think of no better witness to support the truth of this – that I have never charged any fee – than *my own poverty*.

[Socrates holds his arms apart from the sides of his frayed and sooty *chiton* and cloak for a moment.]

And it might seem odd, perhaps, that I go out of my way and

put so much effort into giving you advice about virtue and right living on a one-to-one basis, ... [Visuals of: Anytus standing on an outdoor *bēma*, addressing several thousand men in the amphitheater of the Athenian Assembly; then Lycon standing on the same *bēma* and addressing a different gathering of the Assembly, while the following is heard spoken:] but when it comes to the affairs of the state I do not go through the trouble to appear before the Assembly and provide you with any public recommendations. [Return to Socrates on the *bēma* of the courtroom.] ... The reason for this is something you have heard me speak about many times before in many places throughout our city: a communication from the spirit world that comes to me, ... [Socrates directs his gaze at Meletus as he recalls his opponent's use of the term "things" in reference to it, as if Socrates had a pantheon of strange entities he worshipped.] ... which Meletus certainly made a mockery of in his charges against me. ... [He returns his gaze to the jury members.] ... This communication – the type of voice I experience – has been coming to me over and over again ever since I was a child. And whenever it comes, it always turns me away from a course of action I am about to take but never turns me toward any action that I *ought* to take.

[Cut from the real-time of the courtroom. Flashback to the scene of Socrates talking with several of his companions near the exchange tables in the agora a few days before his trial. He has just finished explaining to Hermogenes how he does not need to prepare a defense because his life of virtue is the best defense that a man can have. Hermogenes asks if Socrates is aware that innocent men have been put to death due to a lack of pity aroused in – and a lack of flattery to – the jury members while making their defense speeches? Socrates replies that he *is* aware of this, but in fact he has tried twice now to begin preparation on a defense and twice now he has been prevented from doing so by his inner voice. Hermogenes expresses surprise that a guardian spirit could be against such a preparation. Socrates asks him if it is really such a surprise that the divine might have decided that death is better for him at this juncture in his life, when the infirmities of old age are approaching? Hermogenes and the others standing around Socrates have no reply for this. Socrates then suggests to them that Apollo could indeed be acting as his personal patron and protector by arranging for his life to be brought to an end at not only the most appropriate age but also in the easiest and most easeful manner. The men surrounding him remain silent. Cut back to the real-time of the courtroom and Socrates on the *bēma*.]

This inner voice, in fact, is what turned me away from entering the realm of politics – and it did an altogether good thing, I tell you, by stopping me in that regard. You must understand, Athenians, that if I had entered the public arena long ago and put my hand into public affairs, *long ago* I would have met my demise and would have then been of no use or benefit to either you or myself.

[Socrates pauses while contemplating his next words. He glances apprehensively through the crowd.]

Now do not get angry at me if I speak the truth, but there is no man whose life will be spared by either you or the people of any other city-state who rightfully opposes his fellow citizens in order to prevent unjust and unlawful acts from occurring in their city. If intending to survive for even a *short* time, the man who truly fights for what is right must live his life as a private citizen and not as a public man. And as ample proof of this, I am going to provide you with – not mere words and speech – but with something you value much more: *actions taken*. Listen carefully to what has happened to me and how I acted, so you can judge for yourselves that I would never, due to fear of death, yield to anyone who wanted me to act beyond my better judgment and against what is just – not even when failure to comply meant *my life itself was at stake.*

[Socrates' gaze is pulled downward. Cut to the herald as he slides two more wooden rings across the horizontal pole of his device. Only two rings remain at the opposite end – the last two *choes* of time. Cut back to Socrates on the platform as he lifts his eyes from the wooden rings to his judges.]

Courtroom testimonials, I know, are common and tedious – and often crudely used to sway the jury, – but what I am about to tell you is both relevant and true. I have only held office once in our fair city, Athenians, and that was as a member of the Council of Five Hundred. While I was performing my civic duties during this term, the men of my own district, Antiochis, were presiding as the ruling committee when you passed the notorious resolution concerning the ten generals of the sea battle at Arginusae. ... [Visual of this battle from far above the waters, with dozens of Spartan and Athenian triremes in close contact, many of them maneuvering to ram the hulls of their enemy's ships, many others on fire, with numberless projectiles flying back and forth between the vessels, while the following is heard spoken:] As you no doubt recall, these were the naval commanders who did not rescue the survivors of the battle and failed to collect the bodies of the fallen from the sea, [Cut back to Socrates on the *bēma*] ... and the resolution declared that the ten of them should be tried *as a group* instead of individually – which was against the law, as you all came to agree later on. But at that time I was the sole presiding officer who opposed this and, not wanting anything unjust to be done, I cast my vote against the resolution and nullified it. And even though the orators of the Assembly were on the verge of declaring me unfit for office and having me impeached and arrested, and even though so many of you were calling out and crying out for this to happen to me as well, I still believed I had to take a firm and fearless stance on the side of law and justice and face the risk of being put in chains or put to death rather than side with you when you were so eager to commit a crime against justice.

[Socrates glares disapprovingly at the jurymen and spectators as he nods his head several times.]

This incident took place during a time of democracy in our city, but another one in which I was personally involved occurred during a time of oligarchy, in those difficult days right after the War. The Thirty Tyrants summoned me and four others to the Rotunda, … [Visual from behind of Socrates entering the Rotunda – the circular city hall of Athens – and standing beside the four other men, also only seen from behind, while the following is heard spoken:] where they assigned us the task of going to Salamis and arresting Leon of Salamis – a man of good standing among the democrats – so that he could be brought to Athens to be executed [Cut back to the view of the *bēma*] … Many times during their reign the Thirty ordered others to carry out such heinous acts for them, wishing to implicate as many of us as possible in their crimes and guilt. And on this occasion I truly did demonstrate through my actions, and not mere words, that as far as death was concerned – and if not too blunt to express it this way, – *I could not care less*. What matters to me above all else is that I never carry out any unjust or impious act. Even the rule of the Thirty, as strong and bloodthirsty as it was, could not strike enough fear into my heart to make me do something I knew to be wrong. When the five of us came out from the Rotunda, my four compatriots set off for Salamis and arrested Leon, while I set off for my home. … [Visual at a distance of Socrates and the four others exiting the Rotunda, with Socrates breaking away from them and setting off in a different direction, while the following is heard spoken:] And most likely I would have been put to death for this, if the oligarchy had not been so quickly overthrown, just eight months after being placed into power. [Visual at a distance of the four compatriots walking away from the Rotunda as one of them suddenly stops and turns around to look back at Socrates. Cut to a close-up of the man – *it's Meletus*, – while the following is heard spoken:] And as witnesses to this – to my refusal to hunt down a decent man at the behest of the tyrants, – there are many men here who can attest to this.

[Cut back to Socrates on the *bēma*, his head turned toward the bench for the prosecution. Cut to that bench, with Meletus staring threateningly back at him. Cut back to Socrates on the platform as he returns his gaze to the jury.]

Athenians, do you think that I would have lived so many years if I had devoted myself to politics? Do you think that if I had defended justice day in and day out in a manner worthy of a virtuous man – considering this defense to be of the greatest importance, as any man should – that I would have lasted so long? Not a chance, Athenians, and neither would any other man of my make. Throughout my life whatever I have done in public – whatever words spoken, decisions made, actions taken – you will find that I am the same man with the same words and decisions and actions in my private life; and I have never – publicly or privately – condoned or made the slightest excuse for any unjust act committed by anyone, whoever he might be ... [Images of: Alcibiades, youthful and attractive, the notorious traitor of the Athenians during the War; then Critias, middle-aged and stern, one of the Thirty Tyrants, and the one most known for being the cruelest, while the following is heard spoken:] – and this includes anyone my attackers claim to be past or present students of mine. [Cut back to the *bēma*] ... I have been a teacher to no one; but at the same time, if anyone has ever wanted to hear me speak and hear how I go about conducting my investigations, I have never held back or turned anybody away, young or old – taking no fee to speak with me, refusing no one because of no fee. I offer myself freely and equally to rich and poor alike, for whatever inquiry they like. Anyone who wants to find out what I have to say on any given topic can do so by engaging me in conversation and answering my usual line of questioning. Now whether the people who talk with me become the better for this or not, it would be wrong to think I could be held responsible for that. I have never promised anybody any lessons or instruction, nor ever taught any. And if anyone claims that he has heard or learned about something from me in private that nobody else has ever heard me say – as if I do not speak openly and equally to all, – you can be certain that he is *full of lies*.

[Socrates glares firmly out at the crowd for a moment. He then relaxes his features and glances around the room in an inquisitive manner.]

So why in the world do young men enjoy spending so much time with me? ... [He points his hand at the jury.] ... You have heard why, Athenians, because I have been completely honest with you: they enjoy listening to men being examined by me – especially men who believe themselves to be wise and knowledgeable in some respect but, as I make clear, are actually *not*. ... [He nods his head with a gentle smile on his face.] ... Young men do find this rather amusing. And as I have explained, the god Apollo is the one who assigned me to perform this task – which he has revealed to me through oracles and dreams and in every way that any god-given fate has ever been revealed for a man to follow.

[Socrates pauses as his eyes lift up toward the windows that run along the upper back wall of the courtroom. Cut to a view of the windows, with the silhouette of a bird perched on a sill, its outline sharp and black against the luminous sky. Cut from the real-time of the courtroom. Flashback to the scene of Socrates speaking with several companions in the agora a few days before his trial. Hermogenes asks Socrates what the nature of the charge of impiety is that's being brought against him. Socrates tenses his brows and asks how in the world can the inner voice that he experiences be described as an impiety? He glares at the men around him, who have no reply. He tells them that there are a great number of people who trust in bird-calls and prophets to foresee the future – and aren't these examples of voices, of communications from the spirit world? The men surrounding him nod. Socrates then mentions the priestess at the oracle of Delphi – does she not relate communications she receives from a divine voice that comes to her? The men surrounding Socrates nod again. He tells his companions that while so many people listen to birds and prophets and oracles, he listens to the communication that occurs inside himself – and by openly and accurately claiming it to be from the spirit world, what makes this claim any more impious than any of the others? His companions have no response to this. Cut back to the real-time of the courtroom and Socrates on the *bēma* as his gaze returns to the level of his judges.]

That this task of mine – my divine fate, Athenians, – is *not* a bad and corrupting influence on the young, the truth of this can be easily tested. If I do in fact corrupt young men, then those whom I have already led to ruin – being older now and realizing that in their youth I counseled them in a harmful way, – they certainly could come up before you now to publicly accuse me and have me punished. Or if these men do not wish to do so themselves, one of their family members here could do so for them. Any of their fathers or brothers or any other relative, they should right here and right now recall how bad my effect has been on their own kith and kin – what horrid injuries I am responsible for – and demand vengeance. ... [Socrates glances around the room, locating many of the faces he has made note of up to this point in his speech.] ... I see many of their fathers who are here, at any rate, and who could do so. ... [He points his palm at the bench for the defense. Visual of the eldest man there, who is seated next to one of the young men – not the one with broad shoulders, but the other, – while the following is heard spoken:] First of all Crito is right here, my same age and from the same district of Attica as me, who is the father of Critobulus. [Cut back to Socrates as he directs his hand up at the spectator area at the back of the court. With each of the following names, the direction of his hand moves throughout the crowd spread out in front of him, to both jurymen and spectators.] ... I also see Lysanias from the district of Sphettos, the father of Aeschines. And Antiphon of Cephisus is there, the father of Epigenes. Just as well, many men are here whose brothers often spent their time with me in conversations and philosophy. For instance, Nicostratus, the son of Theozotides and the brother of Theodotus – who has since passed on and, because of this, could not possibly have asked his brother to support me in court. And I see Paralus is here, the son of Demodocus, whose brother was Theages, who has also passed away. And there is Adimantus, son of Aristo, ... [Socrates turns to indicate the defense bench again with his hand. Visual close-up of the young man with the broad shoulders and penetrating gaze seated there, while the following is heard spoken:] whose brother Plato is also right here. [Cut back to Socrates on the *bēma* as he directs his hand at the spectator area:] And Aeantodorus is here as well, [He then points back at the bench for the defense. Visual close-up of the man in his forties seated there, while the following is heard spoken:] the brother of Apollodorus. [Cut back to the view of Socrates on the speaker's platform as he lowers his arm.] ...

70

And many others are here that I could point out to you, men whom Meletus most certainly *could have* and *should have* brought forth as witnesses during his speech – but if it slipped his mind to do so, right now I will allow him to bring any of them forward. ... [Socrates turns to face the bench for the prosecution.] ... I yield the speaker's platform here and now to let him tell us if he has any testimony from any of these men which he would like to present to the court.

> [Socrates stops and waits. Cut to the juror in charge of the *clepsydra* as he holds the plug for the copper spout toward the trickle of water. Cut next to a close-up of Meletus, angrily glaring back at Socrates. Cut then to a view of the two of them – Socrates on the speaker's platform, Meletus on the prosecution bench – staring at each other for several tense moments. Socrates then turns toward the jury area to see if anyone has stood up to speak. Cut to a view from the platform to show that no one has. Cut back to the juror in charge of the *clepsydra* as he lowers his hand away from the copper spout, allowing the trickle of water and time to continue unabated. Return to Socrates on the *bēma*.]

But as you see, Athenians, just the opposite is the case. They are ready and willing to help *me* rather than Meletus – *me the corrupter*, the one who does terrible things to their very own family members, as Meletus and Anytus have warned you. The victims of my terrible actions – the men that I have brought to ruin, – they might have their reasons for keeping silent and helping me, whatever they might be, but what about their older and uncorrupted relatives? What other reason could they have for helping me now except for the one that is correct and just: they know as well as Meletus does that they are getting *nothing but lies from him and the truth from me*?

> [Socrates glances about the room with an air of vindi-

cation. He then stands still on the platform, his eyes directed straight ahead but inwardly turned. The trickle from the *clepsydra* becomes briefly amplified. After a few moments, his eyes blink away the empty stare and the gleam returns to his bulbous eyes. He glances matter-of-factly around the courtroom.]

Concluding Remarks

Socrates

Well then, Athenians, of all the arguments and anecdotes I could give you today – other ones which failed to come to mind being likely of a similar kind, – the ones I have now given should suffice in proving that I have done nothing wrong. ... [Socrates searches through the faces in front of him.] ... And it might be, now, that someone here is feeling a bit agitated at the recollection of his own actions before a court of law, especially if he happened to be involved in a case of less importance than my own, and recalls how he begged and beseeched the court with a display of children and tears in order to garner the utmost sympathy and support, or brought forth any number of others to plead on his behalf, such as his other family members and friends – but here *I* stand without having done any of these things, and without any intention of doing them, all while running the risk of *the ultimate punishment*, as it could certainly be called. And with this in mind you might take a harsh and unsympathetic stance against me – angered at a defense without any tears or family members, – and you might cast your vote with this anger raging inside of you. ... [Socrates glances quickly throughout the room.] ... If any of you do happen to be like this – I do not truly expect it, but just in case, – I would consider it quite right of me to address such rage by saying that: "I too, my good man, indeed have relatives of my own, since, in the words of Homer, I am neither 'from an oak nor from a rock' but have been born from human beings. So I do have relatives, of course, and sons as well. Three of them: one a teenager already and two boys. But all the same, I have not brought them here with me to place them on display in a court of law for the purpose of begging and beseeching you to cast your vote for my acquittal." And why won't I do such a thing? Not because I do not honor you, Athenians, or have no concern for what you would like to see – and *expect* to see – from a man on trial.

[Socrates takes a moment to inspect the faces and reactions of the jurors. As he resumes speaking, he does so in the loftiest of tones.]

Whether or not I can stand here serenely and at ease in the face of death, that is a different question; but with regard to the honor of *my* reputation and *yours* and of the *city as a whole*, it does not seem proper to me to make a show of tears or children, especially at my stage in life and with the reputation that I have attained, whether true or false. Whichever it is, people have come to believe – and the reputation has prevailed – that Socrates differs from most men and, in one way or another, *surpasses them*.

[Cut to a section of jurors, several of whom have expressions of strong disagreement on their faces. Return to Socrates.]

If any of you who are thought of in this same manner – excelling in wisdom or bravery or in any other virtue at all – were to act in such a way as to induce the pity of a court, what a disgrace that would be. But I have often heard of men of this sort – well-known for their high-standing – who, when they come before a court, engage in unbelievable behavior as if fearing they will suffer something horrible if they die or, even more unbelievable, as if *immortality awaits them if they are not put to death that day.* ... [A look of rebuke takes shape on his face.] ... To my mind, these men bring so much disgrace to the city that a foreigner could easily believe that Athenian men who excel in virtue – that class of men that foreigners themselves judge to be most fit for political offices and other types of esteemed positions in their own cities – are lacking in the very virtue of *manliness itself.* Any of us men of Athens with any type of honorable reputation should never commit such disgraceful acts in court; and if one of us does, it is up to the rest of us to bring it to a halt and make it very clear that we are much more likely to condemn a man for staging such pitiful spectacles – turning the courtroom into a theater and the city into a laughing-stock – than for making a restrained and dignified defense.

[Socrates glares for several moments around the courtroom, nodding his head resolutely.]

Apart from the question of reputation, Athenians, I in no way think it proper for a man on trial to beg or beseech the jury or to be acquitted *because of* such behavior. A man on trial is duty-bound to inform the court with complete honesty and to persuade the jurors with the soundness of reason. A jury member does not sit as a judge in court for the purpose of dispensing favors at the cost of justice – but for making judgment *in accordance with it.* He has not sworn to the oath of the Athenian juror so that he will do anyone any favors out of sympathy or kindness of heart but so he will make his judgment based solely on the law. And because of this, those of us who speak before the court should not accustom those of you who sit as judges into breaking your oaths, or allow you to fall into such a habit on your own, since neither one of us would be acting piously. And with this in mind, Athenians, none of you should expect me to do anything in front of you that I do not believe to be good and honorable or in line with what is just and pious – above all, by Zeus, when I am on trial today for *impiety*, accused of not believing in the gods of our city by Meletus here. If I were to succeed in persuading you to my side by begging and beseeching you – forcing you to break with what you have sworn an oath to, – that would be just the same as if I were to teach you not to believe in gods or to have contempt for religion. By acting out such a defense I would end up entirely *prosecuting myself* for not believing there to be gods or workings of the divine – which is far from the truth, since I *am* a believer, Athenians, and in a far truer sense than any of my accusers.

[Cut to the copper spout of the *clepsydra*. The trickle of water comes to a stop, with several last drops falling into the bottom jar. Cut next to a view from the *bēma* of the three court officials as the herald slides the last two wooden rings across the horizontal pole of his contraption. He lifts his palm and announces that the twelve *choes* of time for the defendant are now complete. Return to Socrates on the platform as he lifts his eyes resignedly from the herald to his judges.]

So now I place myself into your hands – and those of the god Apollo – to pass your judgment in whichever way will be of the most benefit to both you and me.

[Pull back to a view of the *bēma* with the benches at each side. Socrates somberly steps to the edge of the platform, descends it and rejoins his companions on the bench for the defense. He takes his seat between the elderly Crito and the young Plato, and immediately all of the men seated on the bench – Plato, Socrates, Crito, Critobulus, Apollodorus, and Chaerecrates –

75

break into a discussion. The courtroom fills with the sounds of a hundred other simultaneous discussions breaking out. The court herald stands up – as seen from behind, – mounts the *bēma* and lifts his palms. The conversations tone down into whisperings. He asks if there is anyone who challenges the testimony that was presented by the defendant. No one replies. The herald then announces that the defense has rested its case and the jurors will now cast their votes for the verdict. He informs them that they are to remain seated until their section letter is called and that they are *not* to discuss their decisions with anyone while waiting for their turn to vote. He then descends the platform. Cut to the court clerk, who picks up the low circular container at his feet, places it in his lap, rolls up the sheets of papyrus on his writing table, lifts the lid to the container, places the documents inside of it, replaces the lid and stands up with it in his hands.]

The Vote for the Verdict

[Cut to a view from the ceiling above the three court officials, with the *bēma* and the first third of the jury seating area visible. The herald motions toward several men seated in the front row – jurors who have been assigned the task of courtroom assistants for the day – and instructs them to place the chairs, the writing table and the device with the wooden rings on the *bēma*. As they do, dozens of court spectators descend the staircases at the edges of the jury seating area and begin exiting the courtroom through one of the two guarded doorways in opposite corners of the room. The herald directs the assistants to bring two waist-high stands to the area where the court officials had been sitting. Each stand has a circular top a meter in diameter with a wicker basket on top of it containing five hundred *psēphoi* – small bronze wheel-shaped voting tokens. The assistants lift up the token-stands one at a time from their storage area against the wall near the water-clock and carefully carry them to the center of the court. The herald then directs them to bring the two large voting urns – one wooden, one bronze – to the area immediately in front of the *bēma*. As they do, cut to a view of the *bēma* from the level of mid-court, showing the token-stands near the foot of the stair-ways, the voting urns in front of the speaker's plat-form, and the magistrate and court clerk seated on their chairs on the speaker's platform. The herald at-taches wicker-plaited funnels to the top of each voting urn – funnels which narrow into a space large enough to only allow one *psēphos* to pass through at a time.

[The herald stands in the area between the token-stands and voting urns and calls for the jurors to listen carefully to the voting instructions. He points his hand at the stands and tells them that when their section let-ter is announced they will come down and be given one voting token from each stand. He picks up a *psēphos* from each pile and holds them up, one in each hand. He explains that the *psēphoi* are wheel-shaped discs made of bronze with a short axle going through the center of the wheel. One set of discs has a pierced axle which can be seen through – the example of which he continues holding up, lowering his other arm, – and this is the disc used for *a vote of guilty*. The other set of voting tokens has axles which are solid. He holds up the example and tells them that the solid axle is used for *a vote of not guilty*. He repeats that they will receive one of each and, after taking them in hand, they are to proceed to the voting urns. The herald explains that they must hold the voting discs by the axle between their finger and thumb so that no one can see which vote they cast or discard. He demonstrates by holding a token between his finger and thumb and stepping backward toward the voting urns. He tells them that the bronze urn is for the verdict and the wooden urn is for the token not used. He instructs them to place their hand into the top of the funnel – while demonstrating with the funnel on top of the bronze urn – and drop their *psēphos* into it. He pulls his hand out of the funnel – the example token still clasped by the axle between his finger and thumb – and steps to the wooden urn and tells them to discard the other *psēphos* into it in the same fashion. Once they have voted, he instructs them, they may exit the courthouse for the remainder of time it takes for the vote to be completed and counted, but no juror is allowed to leave the gated confines of the courthouse grounds. They may *not*, he stresses, enter into the agora, but they may purchase food and drink from the vendors on the other side of the gate. His final instruction to them is that once the voting process has been completed, they must return to the same lettered seating section in which they are currently seated.

[The herald turns around and asks for witnesses from both benches to approach the voting urns. Anytus, Lycon and Meletus stand up and take positions near the urns. Plato and Critobulus – the two young men on Socrates' bench – stand up and station themselves nearby as well. The herald looks to the magistrate seated above the urns, who motions for the vote to begin. The herald turns around to face the jury and announces that section alpha will now come down to vote. Cut to a view of the jury seating area as seen from behind the court magistrate and clerk on the *bēma*. Fifty men stand up in the far back of the left-side trapezoidal seating section. They shuffle along the wooden benches and begin to descend the stairways on each side of the seating area toward the token-stands at the center of the court. Cut to the assistants. As the jurors begin to file past, they hand them one token from each wicker basket, repeating the terms "guilty" and "not guilty" after every few hand-offs. Cut to the bronze voting urn as the first juror approaches. While holding his voting *psēphos* between his finger and thumb, he places his hand into the top of the funnel. The sound of bronze hitting bronze is heard – *kux*.

[Cut forward in time to the *bēma* with both benches in view. Meletus is standing at its center; Anytus and Lycon are seated on the wooden bench behind him. He's poised with his arm rigidly aimed at the bench for the defense, his bird of prey eyes glaring fervidly at the jury. After a few intense moments, he relaxes his arm and lets it dangle at his side. Anytus and Lycon then stand up, and Anytus leads as the three of them descend the platform and return to their seats on the bench for the prosecution. The herald mounts the platform and announces that the defendant will now be given two *choes* of time to propose a counter-penalty. Socrates rises and walks toward the *bēma* as the herald descends it. Cut to a close-up of his rough-soled feet as they scrape against the three steps of the platform. Cut next to the *clepsydra* in the corner. The juryman in charge of it lifts up the lower jar and pours its six liters – two *choes* of water, approximately twelve minutes of time – back into the upper jar. He replaces the lower jar and unplugs the copper spout above it. The trickle of water and time begins once again. Cut back to Socrates on the *bēma*, without anyone or anything else in view. He glances calmly out at the jury members, his large eyes shining.]

Proposal of a Counter-penalty

Socrates

I have no anger or ill-will at what has just happened – at your vote for my condemnation, Athenians, – and of the many reasons I could give for this reaction of mine, chief among them is that the outcome was not unexpected. What I *am* surprised about is the tally of the votes for me and against. … [View from above the *abax* – the stone table used for counting the voting discs. It consists of two identical halves, both with twenty-five columns of twenty slots each. Visuals of: the courtroom assistants pouring the contents of the bronze voting urn into a wicker basket on top of a wide-rimmed stand on one side of the *abax*; the men picking up the *psēphoi*, examining their axles, and placing the ones that are pierced into the slots on one side of the *abax* and the ones that are solid into the slots on the opposite side; then a view of the completed vote count, with 280 pierced-axle *psēphoi* on one side and 220 solid-axle *psēphoi* on the other, while the following is heard spoken:] I did not think the votes against me would win by such a slim margin. I had expected it to be much wider. As it is, if only thirty of the votes had been cast differently, I would have been acquitted. [Cut back to Socrates on the *bēma*. He gives a slight tilt to his head.] … And in a sense, if you take Meletus and a third of his vote, I *have* been acquitted – and not just that, but anyone can see that if Anytus and Lycon had not come to court with Meletus to accuse me, he would right now be owing the penalty of one thousand drachmas for not receiving at least one-fifth of the total votes from the jury.

[Socrates pauses, face aglow. Cut to a sector of jurors, with very few of their faces glowing back. Cut back to Socrates as his mirthfulness transits into solemnity. He extends his arm toward Meletus.]

This man proposes the death penalty for me. Well then, Athenians, should I propose a counter-penalty to you? Or is it obvious that this penalty is sufficient?

[Socrates pauses and glances around the room.]

Is it, though? What do I deserve to suffer, or how much do I deserve to pay, because I could not lead a quiet and humble life? What do I deserve because I have not cared about the things that most people care about, such as making money or tending to household affairs or carrying out the duties of a general or giving speeches at the Assembly – or cared about any of the other public offices or secret clubs or political factions that have come and gone in our city? What do I deserve because I truly believed myself to be too reasonable and fair-minded to enter into these affairs and, *while acting on behalf of justice*, being capable of lasting very long?

[Socrates pauses for several moments before again assuming his highest-standing tone.]

I did not follow a path in life where, once I reached my station, I would have been of no benefit to either you or myself. Instead I followed a path – a god-given path, allowing *Apollo* to station me – where I met with you separately and privately and did you as much benefit as I possibly could. This path I took – the one of striving to convince you not to care for your everyday affairs before you have taken care of your *moral and mental excellence*, and not to be concerned about the everyday affairs of the state before the *excellence of the state itself*, and to use this approach when it comes to any and all other matters, – what do I deserve for following this path in life and being a man such as this?

[Socrates glances inquisitively around the room, as if expecting the correct answer to be blurted out. His face then brightens as he provides the answer himself.]

A *reward*, Athenians.

[Cut from the real-time of the courtroom. Flashback to Socrates in the agora talking with his companions a few days before his trial. He has just suggested that Apollo may be doing him a favor by arranging for him to be so easefully put to death at this stage in his life. Hermogenes tells Socrates that he cannot bear to hear him or anyone else speak so favorably of being condemned to death. Socrates responds by describing old age as a terrible pit of illness and troubles that too many people fall into, and he will most certainly not go out of his way during his trial in order to enable himself to fall into such a pit. He confides to Hermogenes and the other men surrounding him that if he ends up offending the jury by making clear to them the ways he has been blessed by the gods and by expressing the true opinion he has of himself, he will prefer their punishment of death rather than beg for his life. A couple of the men around him shake their heads in disagreement. Socrates counters this by resolutely stating that any attempt to escape death – in particular by begging in a slavish manner – can only be rewarded with a *much meaner and lesser existence*. Cut back to the real-time of the courtroom and Socrates on the *bēma*, eyes still gleaming.]

Yes, *something good*, if the consequences of my actions are to fit the actions themselves, and if I am to truly receive my so-called just desserts.

[The courtroom bursts into outrage. One man shouts out that this is unbelievable impudence; another man yells that this is a total disgrace to justice; and other men, mostly garbed in the earthier-colored *chitons*, hurl far worse abuse. Socrates stands on the *bēma*, nodding his head. Cut to the view from the *bēma* as the herald rises up, turns around and lifts both of his palms while calling for silence. The exasperation begins to die down. Cut back to Socrates, who patiently waits for the commotion to lessen to a level in which he's able to speak without raising his voice. Once it does, he calmly continues.]

And it should be a reward that not only fits my actions but *me myself*. So what is appropriate for a poor yet well-meaning man – a benefactor to both you and the state – who wishes to lead a life free from toil for the sake of encouraging and ele-vating you?

[One man shouts out that exile is appropriate. Another man shouts out that death is much more appropriate, with cheers of agreement throughout the crowd.]

Men of Athens, nothing could be deemed more fit for such a man than to be *fed for life at state expense in city hall.*

[The courtroom once again bursts into outrage. One man yells that this is utter nonsense; another man cries out that they are all being insulted on purpose; and another shouts out that *this* is a true example of a child-ish prank. Socrates stands patiently on the speaker's platform. Cut to the view of the seating area as seen from the speaker's platform as the herald stands up again and turns around to address the raging patch-work of differently-hued *chitons*. A number of jurors are on their feet, making threatening gestures and curses at Socrates. The herald raises both palms and demands for there to be silence in the court. Many of those standing sit down, but the outcries continue. The herald demands silence again. Cut back to Socrates as the volume of the outburst lessens. He waits for it to decrease to the point where he can speak in his normal tone of voice. Once it does, he continues in earnest.]

I think this reward is far more appropriate for me and what I have done than for any of you who may be receiving free meals due to a single horse or a pair of horses or a chariot of horses at the Olympic games. An Olympic victor has not the need for sustenance at state expense, while I most certainly do; and an Olympic victory makes us only *seem to be* happy and in high spirits, while the high-spiritedness I encourage *truly makes one happy*. So on account of this, if I had to propose a penalty in measure with justice – one on equal footing with what I have done, – I would propose just that: to receive free meals for life in the Rotunda.

[A final wave of grumbles and jeers respond to the suggestion, but for the most part the energy behind the outrage has been spent.]

By saying this, some of you might think I am speaking much like I did about displays of pity and pleading in court – with too much audacity and too little concern for what you would like to hear from me. But this is not the case, Athenians. I speak this way due to my whole-hearted belief that I have never willingly done any wrong to anyone – even though I am failing right now to persuade you of this because of what little time I have been given to discuss the matter in front of you.

[Cut to the *clepsydra*. The bottom jar has reached the level of being roughly half full. Return to Socrates on the *bēma*.]

I am certain that if we had a law to judge capital cases over a period of several days instead of merely just one – such as they have in other city-states, – you *would* be persuaded. But as things stand, it is no easy task to release you from such a deeply-ingrained and widespread prejudice in such a small amount of time and clear my name. And being, as I am, convinced that I do no wrong to anyone, I certainly have no intention of *doing anything wrong to myself*. I cannot be expected to scheme against myself and claim that I deserve something horrible to happen to me or to propose such a punishment as that for myself. Why should I? Due to a fear that I might experience the thing that Meletus proposes as my penalty – the very thing that I confessed to have no idea whether it is a blessing or a curse?

[Socrates glares out defiantly at the crowd for several moments. His features then relax as he takes on an air of contemplation.]

How about this, then: I choose something instead of death, something I know for certain to be bad, and propose *that* as my penalty – like imprisonment? … [He scans the faces in the crowd.] … But then, why should I pass my days like that, being a slave to the whims of the Eleven, a prison authority whose members and edicts are constantly changing? … [He quickly scans the faces again.] … Well then, how about proposing the penalty of a fine and confining myself to jail until I can pay it off? … [He makes another scan for reactions.] … But

85

this harkens back to the same thing I was saying earlier, how I do not have the money for fines or anything else. So then, should I suggest exile? ... [Socrates nods his head.] ... Most likely you would accept that as a penalty for me. ... [He stops nodding and speaks with complete seriousness.] ... How tightly I must be clinging onto dear life, Athenians, if I lack the clarity of mind to see that you, my own fellow citizens, cannot put up with my investigations and examinations and exhortations – which have become such a burden to you and riled up so much resentment that you are now searching for a way to rid yourselves of them, – but that people in other city-states will somehow *tolerate them with ease*? This is far from ever happening, Athenians. And what a wonderful life I would lead, a man of my age, departing from Athens and roaming for the rest of my days from city to city, constantly being driven out and banished from each one of them. I am quite aware that wherever I might go the young men will gather around me and listen to whatever I have to say, just as they do here. Even if I somehow managed to keep them away from me and prevented them from joining in my discussions, these youths – of their own accord and out of vengeance – would convince their elders to have me banished. Or if I did *not* keep them away from me and spoke with them like I do the young men here, their fathers and family members would have me banished for their sake.

[Cut to a sector of jurors, several of whom are nodding their heads in agreement. Cut back to Socrates as his eyes glide through the crowd.]

Now perhaps someone here might say: "Socrates, after departing from us into exile, you would surely be able to lead your life in a quiet and humble manner by engaging in *no more philosophical discussions*, wouldn't you?" ... [A look of exasperation spreads across his face.] ... This in itself is the most difficult point to convey to some of you. If I tell you that leading

86

such a life would be disobedient to the god Apollo and, because of that, I cannot keep my mouth and my mind silent, you will take it for granted that I am being ironic – making some type of subtle joke – and you will refuse to believe me. Or if, instead, I tell you what a great benefit it truly is for a man to spend his days engaging in discussions about virtue and the other topics you often hear me talking about, and how truly rewarding it is to search within myself and others – *an unexamined life being hardly worth living* – you will believe me even less. And even though all of this is true – and I insist that it is, Athenians, – it is not easy to convince you of that. So I will not propose exile as a counter-penalty. At the same time, I have difficulty thinking of myself as being deserving of anything bad or being worthy of any type of punishment – I simply am not used to looking at myself that way. If I had any money, I would have proposed a fine of as much as I owned and could pay – which would be no true harm, all the same. But as it is, right now I do not have any wealth to speak of, unless you would like me to propose a fine of as much as I could pay if given a little time. In that case, I could probably manage to scrape together one mina of silver for you. This is the amount, then, that I propose as my counter-penalty.

[An uproar breaks out. Some bellow out in mocking laughter and others hurl insults at the lack of proportion between the sum and the penalty of death – one mina of silver being equal to one hundred drachmas, and one hundred drachmas being equal to one hundred days of labor at minimum wage. Pull back to a wider view of the *bēma*, including the bench for the defense. Plato has his hand raised and is calling out to Socrates. Socrates looks over at him. Plato lifts his other hand in order to flash his ten digits three times; he then indicates certain men seated on the bench. Socrates looks back at the jurymen and spectators, who are still growling. He holds up his palm.]

Men of Athens.

[As they quiet down, he points his palm at the bench for the defense.]

Plato here, along with Crito and Critobulus and Apollodorus, tell me to make it *thirty* minas, with the four of them guaranteeing the sum. So I propose that as my penalty now – *thirty minas of silver*, – and you can certainly trust that these men will be reliable guarantors of the money.

[Without any further concern, Socrates turns away from the jury, descends the platform and returns to his seat between Plato and Crito. Several jeers are thrown at him as he takes his seat, including one jury member who shouts that punishing *Socrates' friends* is not why they are here today. The herald steps onto the platform, raises a palm and announces that the jurors will now vote for one of the two punishments: either the fine of thirty minas of silver or the penalty of death. He informs them that the voting process for the punishment will be identical to the voting process for the verdict, except that the *psēphoi* with the pierced axles will now represent *a vote for death*, and the *psēphoi* with the solid axles will represent *a vote for the fine of thirty minas*. He also informs the jurors that after casting their vote they will hand their payment tokens to the court clerk, who will disburse their pay of half a drachma for volunteering for jury duty today. After receiving their pay, the herald continues, their duties here will be complete, and they may leave the courthouse; or, if they would prefer to remain till the end of the court session, they may do so and sit wherever they would like. The herald then directs his voice toward the upper back of the courtroom and announces to the spectators that after the vote is complete and the jurors who wish to remain have seated themselves, they may sit in any seating space which is unoccupied. He then motions for the courtroom assistants to once again rise up in order to prepare for the vote. Cut to the *clepsydra* in the corner. The jury member in charge of it is standing next to his tripod stool with a drinking amphora clasped in his hands, tilting it by its two handles as a trickle of water flows out from the spout and into his mouth.

[Cut forward in time to a view from above the *abax*. It contains 360 *psēphoi* with pierced axles in the slots on one half of its top and 140 *psēphoi* with solid axles on its other half. Cut next to a view of the herald standing on the *bēma* as seen from the back rows of the jury seating area. Roughly three hundred men are scattered about on the wooden benches, with another fifty or so standing in the open space at the center of court and the sides of the speaker's platform. The three chairs for the court officials have been placed between the *bēma* and the prosecution bench – the magistrate and clerk seated in theirs, with two members of the Eleven standing near them, – and the two courtroom guards have been stationed behind the bench for the defense. A hush overtakes the room as everyone's attention becomes focused on the herald. He announces that the vote for punishment is 360 to 140 in favor of the penalty of death – which elicits several praises to Zeus and Apollo from the crowd, – and the defendant is therefore sentenced to death by drinking hemlock. Cut from the real-time of the courtroom and flash forward to Socrates as he grasps the vial of hemlock out of the hand of a prison guard in his cell. A group of his companions are standing around him, a couple of whom place their hands over their faces as he swallows the poison without any hesitation. Socrates then gives the empty vial back to the guard, an air of complete serenity surrounding him. Cut back to the real-time of the courtroom as the men standing around the *bēma* start filing out of the courthouse, talking animatedly among themselves. Anytus, Meletus and Lycon rise up as these men leave, receiving compliments from many of them with grasps of their hands and bright smiles. As they are emptying out of the courtroom, the herald announces that the defendant will be allowed to make a final statement. He then descends the platform and takes his seat next to the magistrate, who resumes his discussion with the members of the Eleven about today's proceedings. The court clerk is seated on the other side of the magistrate, with a sheet of papyrus spread out in front of him on his writing table and a reed quill in his hand, waiting for the official wording of the charges and the warrant for death to be dictated to him. Once the surge of fifty or so men has exited the courtroom, Anytus, Meletus and Lycon retake their seats. Socrates then rises up from the bench for the defense and ascends the speaker's platform. Pull in to a view of Socrates on the *bēma* without anyone or anything else in view.]

Final Words

Socrates

For the sake of a handful of years – or whatever remains of my natural life, Athenians, – you have earned the ill-repute and blame of those who seek to criticize our city. They will say that you have killed Socrates, a wise man – they will call me "wise" whether I am or not, those who look for opportunities to attack you, – and they will say that if you had just waited a short while longer, the punishment you gave him would have occurred of its own accord, since you certainly saw his age and how far along in life he was and that death was near.

[Socrates pauses to examine faces in the crowd, as if scrutinizing friend from foe.]

I do not direct this rebuke at all of you, just at those of you who cast your vote for my death. And I have this to say to you same men as well. You might have it in your minds, Athenians, that I have been convicted due to being at a loss for certain arguments and explanations that could have swayed you and saved my life. This could only be the case if I thought I were compelled to do or say anything, *no matter what*, to escape justice – which is far from the truth with me. I have been convicted – not for a lack of the proper appeals – but for a lack of the proper *brazenness and shamelessness*. I have not succumbed to the tactic of telling you whatever might sound most pleasing to your ears – lamenting and wailing as in a dirge, or doing or saying any number of other things that are beneath me, things that you have heard too many times from too many other men in my situation. ... [He shakes his head.] ... While I was giving my speech I certainly did not think I ought to do anything slavish for you because of the penalty I was facing, and I certainly have no regret about making my defense in the way that I did. I would much rather choose to die with such a defense than to live a life *enslaved to the will of others*. In court or in battle, nobody – including myself – should ever struggle to avoid death by any means possible. ... [Visuals from the Peloponnesian War of: the Athenian victory in Potidaea, with Athenian soldiers – a middle-aged Socrates among them – pursuing the retreating Potidaeans, one of whom has thrown down his weapon and shield and gotten down on his knees in supplication as his enemies overtake him; then the Athenian defeat at the temple to Apollo in Delium, with Boeotians pursuing the retreating Athenians – Socrates among them, – one of whom has thrown down his weapon and shield and gotten down on his knees in supplication as his enemies overtake him, while the following is heard spoken:] In battles it became clear to me again and again that any man might escape death by throwing his armor to the ground and turning on bended knee to those who are chasing after him. Acts such as this, and many other ways of escaping death, exist for any type of danger [Cut back to Socrates on the *bēma*] ... – *if* a man has the heart for doing or saying whatever it takes to stay alive. ... [He tilts his head.] ... But escaping death, Athenians, might not be such a difficult thing to do. A far more difficult thing is to escape *viciousness* – so much swifter is vice than death. The slower of the two has hold of me since I myself am old and slow; the swifter – *vile acts* – has hold of my accusers since they are so much more cunning and quicker of wit.

[Cut to Anytus, Meletus and Lycon, gazing at Socrates indulgently, with vindicated expressions on their faces. Cut back to the *bēma*.]

Here I stand, about to take my leave being sentenced by you to death; here these men sit, being found guilty *by truth* of vice and injustice. I dutifully await my punishment; these men await theirs. I consider this to be quite correct and well within measure – and perhaps, I dare say, even *fated to be.*

[Cut to the court clerk, who is busily writing as the magistrate dictates the phrasing of the charges to him. Cut back to Socrates on the *bēma,* who proceeds in a lofty and prophetic tone.]

And with fate in mind, I would now like to pronounce an oracle to those of you who cast your votes against me, since I am at the point where most men see into the future, being on the verge of death. I declare to those of you who have killed me that *retribution will rebound on you straight after my demise.* A penalty is coming which will give you far more trouble, by Zeus, than the one you have exacted on me. You have penalized me with death in the belief that you will now free yourselves from being examined and being forced to make validations of your lives. But I assure you, very much *the opposite* will occur. People who want to scrutinize your beliefs and actions and analyze your explanations and excuses – there are many people like this out there, unknown to you for so long because of my presence holding them back, … [Socrates briefly glances at the bench for the defense. Cut to a close-up of Plato as his eyes meet Socrates' eyes. Cut back to the *bēma.*] … – they will come at you from out of the woodwork and their number will only increase. I give you fair warning: they will be even more difficult to deal with than I have been – as difficult as they are young, in fact – and you will be all the more agitated and angry. … [He shakes his head decisively.] … If you think that putting men to death is how to go about preventing anyone from criticizing you for not living your life as is best, you are *greatly mistaken.* Handing out the penalty of death does not free you from the scrutiny of others, nor is it even a very effective or good method of stopping that from happening to you. The easiest and most effective way to free yourself from having to make explanations and receiving rebuke is – not cutting short other men's lives – but *constantly*

93

cultivating your soul to be as excellent as possible.

[Socrates pauses for the weight of his words to sink solidly into the minds and souls of all of those present.]

With these words, and with having now pronounced my oracle to those of you who condemn me, I take my leave of you who give me death.

[Cut to a view of the court officials, who are referring to a papyrus in the hands of one member of the Eleven. It contains the laws of Athens concerning impiety and other capital crimes. Cut back to Socrates on the *bēma*.]

As for those of you who voted for my *life*, ... [Socrates steps off of the *bēma* and stands in the space between it and the jury seating area.] ... while the court officials are still preoccupied – and I am not yet taken to that place where, once having arrived, I must die, – I would gladly have a word with you about what has happened today. So remain with me, men, for however long it takes them to complete their business. Nothing prevents us from talking with one another until I am led away. I want to show you – as friends of mine – the meaning of today's proceedings.

[Socrates stops and waits, an expectant gleam in his eyes. Cut to a view of the seating area as seen from behind him. Several dozen men scattered throughout the area stand up to leave – men who do not consider themselves to be a friend of the defendant or who have had enough of his philosophical preachings for the day. They sidle down the wooden benches to the stairways and start filing out of the courthouse, a disgruntled murmur among them. A few of them give spiteful glares at Socrates as they pass him and depart. Cut to the court clerk as the magistrate is dictating the warrant for death to him. Cut then to a front row view of Socrates, standing in front of the speaker's platform. As the last of the men shuffle out, he glances around at the ones who have remained.]

Something remarkable, judges – I am calling you judges now since I would like to address you in a way that you deserve, – something remarkably good has happened to me. It involves the inner signal I have so often received – the one of a spiritual and prophetic nature, – which in the past has always been so close and constant to me, forewarning me even in the smallest or most trivial matters if I am about to make an ill-fated mistake. But today, with what has happened to me – which you see for yourselves how anyone could consider it to be the worst, most ill-fated thing that can happen to a person, and most people *do*, – the divine sign did not warn or oppose me a single time. Not when I was leaving my home early this morning, not while I was walking here to the courthouse, not at any point when I was about to state something in my speech – although in many other discussions and conversations it has stopped me many times from making certain statements while I was speaking. But nowhere today concerning the trial and the charges against me has it opposed me in any way, not in what I did or in what I said. So what do I suppose the reason for this to be? ... [A cheerful expression spreads across his face.] ... I will tell you: what has happened here today – this sentence of death – must surely be *good for me.*

[A gasp is released from many in the crowd. Socrates nods his head.]

Those of us who think of death as something bad, we are apparently making a wrong assumption. And I have fairly substantial proof of this: the signal that has come to me throughout my life – helping me by halting me – would have halted me today if I were *not* about to enter into something good and fortunate for myself.

[Cut to the court clerk as he's drying the fresh ink on the warrant for death with his blotting cloth. Cut back to Socrates as he continues in a philosophical tone.]

Or let's consider it in another way, where we can see how much hope there is that death *is* something good, by making the observation that death is either one of two things. Either it is like nothingness and the dead have no consciousness or perception of anything, or – as followers of Pythagoras and Orpheus tell us – it is actually a type of metamorphosis and a transmigration of the soul from this world to another.

[Socrates pauses thoughtfully.]

If it *is* an unconscious state lacking any awareness whatsoever – like a dreamless sleep where you see and sense nothing, – what a *wonderful boon* death must be. I think anyone, if he had to select a night of sleep that was so deep and sound that he had no dreams and then had to take that night and set it side by side with every other day and night of his life in order to say how many of those days or nights were better and more pleasant, anyone who did this in a thorough fashion – and not just any common man but the great king of Persia himself – would find that the number could be counted *on a single hand*. So if death is something like that – a deep dreamless sleep, – I definitely do call it blissful and a boon, especially since the whole of time seems no longer than a single night.

[Cut to the court magistrate as he signs the first of the documents dealing with the day's proceedings. The two members of the Eleven are standing on each side of him, awaiting their turns to do the same. Cut back to Socrates in front of the *bēma*.]

And as for the other choice, if death is actually a migration from this world to another and what the Pythagoreans and Orphics say is true – that all who have died are in that other world, – what greater benefit than this could there be? If it is true that when someone arrives in Hades, after having left behind the men who *claim* to be judges in this world, he finds himself among those who truly *are* judges – the ones who preside over the underworld, as we are told, like Minos and Rhadamanthys and Aeacus, sons of Zeus; and Triptolemus, the first farmer; and all of the other heroic demi-gods who were men of justice in their mortal lives. Could this migration of the soul be seen as anything less than supremely good? ... [Socrates speaks in his most enthusiastic tone yet.] ... Or how about the opportunity to meet and mingle with Orpheus and Musaeus, and Hesiod and Homer – how many minas of silver would any of you give for such an experience? I am willing to die many times over if this awaits me. Just think of the discussions I could have! ... [Socrates smiles broadly at the thought.] ... It would be far too wonderful for me, especially when I could meet Palamedes and Ajax and any of the other ancient heroes whose deaths were the outcome of unjust judgments and compare my own experiences with theirs – which, for me, would not be an unpleasant thing to do. The greatest boon of all, though, would be to question and examine the men in that world just as I do the men in this one, discovering who among them is truly wise and who among them *thinks* he is wise but is truly not. What price would any of you men pay to have the chance to ask questions of Agamemnon – the one who led the great legions to Troy – or Odysseus or Sisyphus or any of the countless other men and women who could be mentioned?

[Socrates glances around the room, his large eyes beaming. He continues ecstatically.]

To be able to question them, to converse with them, to meet and mingle with them in that other realm – what words are there to describe such bliss? And in that realm they do *not* put anyone to death for questioning or conversing or mingling – nor *could* they. If what we hear is true, they have many reasons for being happier and more light-hearted than we are in this world, but chief among them is that they are all *deathless for the rest of time.*

[Cut to the court clerk as he places the rolled-up warrant for death into the hands of one member of the Eleven. He then places the rolled-up papyrus of the charges against Socrates into the document container in his lap and firmly applies the lid. Cut back to Socrates, whose voice has returned to a measured tone.]

So as for death, judges, you ought to have hope about what awaits you. And one truth to bear in mind is that vice and villainy cannot do true damage to a good man: his soul remains intact and untouched in life and in death, and his concerns are always a concern to the gods. As for *my* present concern, what happened today has not happened by mere chance, and I can clearly see now that death and the release from troubles it brings was the better judgment for me. This explains the silence of the inner sign and why it made no effort to turn me away from anything at any point during the day. And due to this, I am in no way vengeful or angry at any of you who may have condemned me or accused me – even though you had no intention of doing me any benefit but rather of doing me *great harm*, and for that you do deserve blame. But nonetheless I have something to ask of you men, those of you who voted for my death. When my sons have grown and become men, if it becomes clear that they care for wealth or possessions or anything else more than virtue, and if they believe themselves to have amounted to something when in fact they have not, punish them by stinging them in the same way as I have stung you. Openly criticize them for not caring about what they should – *the improvement of their souls* – and for believing themselves to have achieved something when in fact they deserve no praise at all. If you do this, you will have acted justly on my grateful behalf, and on behalf of my sons as well.

[The two courtroom guards approach Socrates and stand on each side of him. With eyes shining, he makes his final statement.]

Well then, the time of departure has arrived – for me to die and for you to live. Which of us is headed down the better course, nobody knows but the gods.

[The guards take hold of Socrates' arms and direct him toward the exit. They let go of him as he complies and starts walking in that direction. Cut to the defense bench, where Socrates' companions are standing, a couple of whom have tears on their faces. Socrates stops as he passes and expresses his surprise at their reaction. He informs them that ever since he was born he has been condemned to die; and, if anything, with the ease of his release from life and the ills of old age that are approaching, his friends ought to be happy for him. Cut to a close-up of Apollodorus, the most sorrowful of the group, who tells Socrates that the most difficult thing for him to bear is to see him being put to death unjustly. Cut to a view of Socrates and Apollodorus standing face to face as Socrates smiles and places his hand on the back of Apollodorus's head. He asks his dearest of friends what he would rather see: him being put to death *un*justly or *justly*? Apollodorus replies with a smile. The guards then take hold of Socrates by the arms again and turn him toward the exit. He resumes walking in that direction. Close with Socrates walking toward the exit, entirely serene and at ease, as his companions and the two members of the Eleven follow him out.]

Texts & Sources

"Extracts from the Oath of an Athenian Juror" is pieced together from Demosthenes, *Against Timocrates*, 149-151, and *Against Eubulides*, 63.

The description of Meletus comes from Plato's *Euthyphro*; the description of Socrates comes from Xenophon's *Symposium*.

The play by Aristophanes is *The Clouds*.

The scene in Anytus's house comes from Plato's *Meno*.

The four flashbacks to the scene in the agora of Socrates talking with his companions a few days before his trial, and the scene at the end of the trial after Socrates' final words, come from Xenophon's version of *The Apology of Socrates*.

Nearly all other flashbacks and scenes from outside the courtroom – as well as most of the interpretations of the text, when siding with an interpretation is required – are based on the notes and commentary in John Burnet's 1924 edition of *Plato's Euthyphro, Apology of Socrates and Crito* (Oxford University Press).

The Greek text I used is the version edited by John Burnet and found in James J. Helm's annotated edition of Plato's *Apology* (Bolchazy-Carducci Publishers, 1999). Helm's edition contains grammatical commentary and a full lexicon, but my ultimate resource for vocabulary was Liddell and Scott's *Greek-English Lexicon* (1883).

Another resource which uses Burnet's edited text of *The Apology* is Tufts University's Perseus Project, www.perseus.tufts.edu, which I constantly referenced for grammar, vocabulary, and the English translation that is provided there (Harold North Fowler's 1914 translation, as found in the Loeb Classical Library edition of *The Apology*).

Two other translations I constantly referenced: Benjamin Jowett's 1907 translation, and the Penguin Classics 1993 edition of *The Last Days of Socrates*, containing Hugh Tredennick's 1954 translation.

The courtroom interior, equipment, and procedures are based on the testimonia in *The Lawcourts of Athens* (American School of Classical Studies at Athens, 1995) as well as the Athenian agora excavation website of the American School of Classical Studies at Athens: www.agathe.gr.com.

Please note that the information on Athenian lawcourts is very slim, so I was forced to take many liberties in order to cinematize the text in this respect. Though the voting process is well described by Aristotle in *The Constitution of the Athenians*, the lay-out of the courtroom – eg. where the *clepsydra* was placed; where the court officials sat; how the court officials and those speaking on the *bēma* were able to keep track of time simultaneously (I invented the herald's twelve-ring device for this); whether there was one *bēma* or two (ie. one for the prosecution, one for the defense); etc. – I had to construct a visual totality from the scraps of information that exist, and it certainly should not be taken as an authentic – or even a very close to authentic – representation. Nobody knows the actual court setting and procedures of Socrates' trial other than the ancient Athenians themselves.

Also note that I have occasionally added words or phrases into the text in order to clarify or expand a point, all for the purpose of making the text as thoroughly comprehensible and complete as possible *without the use of footnotes*.

About the Translator & Cinematizer

Steve Kostecke studied Greek while earning a master's degree in Foreign Language Education (University of Texas, Austin, 1997). Since then he has taught English as a Foreign Language in universities in Japan, Korea, Thailand, and the United States. He is also one of the founders of the Underground Literary Alliance and was its editor-in-chief from 2000 to 2008, during which time he compiled the five editions of the group's literary zine, *Slush Pile*.

CPSIA information can be obtained
at www.ICGtesting.com
Printed in the USA
LVHW041250180619
621592LV00001B/132/P